SHEPHERD'S NOTES

SHEPHERD'S NOTES

When you need a guide through the Scriptures

Jonah/ Zephaniah

BROADMAN
&HOLMAN
PUBLISHERS

Nashville, Tennessee

Shepherd's Notes®—Jonah, Micah, Nahum, Habakkuk and Zephaniah
© 1999
by Broadman & Holman Publishers
Nashville, Tennessee
All rights reserved
Printed in the United States of America

0–8054–9334–4
Dewey Decimal Classification: 224.90
Subject Heading: BIBLE. O.T. JONAH
Library of Congress Card Catalog Number: 99–11546

Library of Congress Cataloging-in-Publication Data
Wright, Paul, 1955-
    Jonah, Micah, Nahum, Habakkuk & Zephaniah / Paul Wright, editor [i.e. author].
        p.   cm. — (Shepherd's notes)
    Includes bibliographical references.
    ISBN 0–8054–9334–4 (pbk.)
    1. Bible. O.T. Jonah—Study and teaching.   2. Bible. O.T. Micah—Studying
and teaching. 3. Bible O.T. Nahum—Studying and teaching.   4. Bible O.T. Habakkuk—Studying and teaching. 5. Bible. O.T. Zephaniah—Study and teaching.
    I. Title.   II. Title: Jonah, Micah, Nahum, Habakkuk, and Zephaniah.   III. Se-
ries
    BS1560.W75   1999
    224'.90—dc21   99–11546
                                                                            CIP

1 2 3 4 5   03 02 01 00 99

CONTENTS

FOREWORD

Dear Reader:

Shepherd's Notes are designed to give you a quick, step-by-step overview of every book of the Bible. They are not meant to be substitutes for the biblical text; rather, they are study guides intended to help you explore the wisdom of Scripture in personal or group study and to apply that wisdom successfully in your own life.

Shepherd's Notes guide you through the main themes of each book of the Bible and illuminate fascinating details through appropriate commentary and reference notes. Historical and cultural background information brings the Bible into sharper focus.

Six different icons, used throughout the series, call your attention to historical-cultural information, Old Testament and New Testament references, word pictures, unit summaries, and personal application for everyday life.

Whether you are a novice or a veteran at Bible study, I believe you will find *Shepherd's Notes* a resource that will take you to a new level in your mining and applying the riches of Scripture.

In Him,

David R. Shepherd
Editor-in-Chief

HOW TO USE THIS BOOK

DESIGNED FOR THE BUSY USER

Shepherd's Notes for Jonah, Micah, Nahum, Habakkuk, and Zephaniah is designed to provide an easy-to-use tool for getting a quick handle on these significant Bible books' important features, and for gaining an understanding of their messages. Information available in more difficult-to-use reference works has been incorporated into the *Shepherd's Notes* format. This brings you the benefits of many advanced and expensive works packed into one small volume.

Shepherd's Notes are for laymen, pastors, teachers, small-group leaders and participants, as well as the classroom student. Enrich your personal study or quiet time. Shorten your class or small-group preparation time as you gain valuable insights into the truths of God's Word that you can pass along to your students or group members.

DESIGNED FOR QUICK ACCESS

Bible students with time constraints will especially appreciate the timesaving features built into the *Shepherd's Notes*. All features are intended to aid a quick and concise encounter with the heart of the messages of Jonah, Micah, Nahum, Habakkuk, and Zephaniah.

Concise Commentary. Short sections provide quick "snapshots" of the themes of these books.

Outlined Text. Comprehensive outlines cover the entire text of Jonah, Micah, Nahum, Habakkuk, and Zephaniah. This is a valuable feature for following each book's flow, allowing for a quick, easy way to locate a particular passage.

Shepherd's Notes. These summary statements or capsule thoughts appear at the close of every key section of the narratives. While functioning in part as a quick summary, they also deliver the essence of the message presented in the sections which they cover.

Icons. Various icons in the margin highlight recurring themes in Jonah, Micah, Nahum, Habakkuk, and Zephaniah, aiding in selective searching or tracing of those themes.

Questions to Guide Your Study. These thought-provoking questions and discussion starters are designed to encourage interaction with the truth and principles of God's Word.

DESIGNED TO WORK FOR YOU

Personal Study. Using the *Shepherd's Notes* with a passage of Scripture can enlighten your study and take it to a new level. At your fingertips is information that would require searching several volumes to find. In addition, many points of application occur throughout the volume, contributing to personal growth.

Teaching. Capsule thoughts designated as "Shepherd's Notes" provide summary statements for presenting the essence of key points and events. Application icons point out personal application of the messages of the books. Historical Context icons indicate where cultural and historical background information is supplied.

Group Study. Shepherd's Notes can be an excellent companion volume to use for gaining a quick but accurate understanding of the messages of these prophetic books. Each group member can benefit from having his or her own copy. The *Note's* format accommodates the study of themes throughout Jonah, Micah, Nahum, Habakkuk, and Zephaniah. Leaders may use its flexible features to prepare for group sessions or use them during group sessions. Questions to guide your study can spark discussion of these prophets and their truths to be discovered in these books.

LIST OF MARGIN ICONS USED IN JONAH, MICAH, NAHUM, HABAKKUK, AND ZEPHANIAH

Shepherd's Notes. Placed at the end of each section, a capsule statement provides the reader with the essence of the message of that section.

Historical Context. To indicate historical information—historical, biographical, cultural—and provide insight on the understanding or interpretation of a passage.

Old Testament Reference. Used when the writer refers to Old Testament passages or when Old Testament passages illuminate a text.

New Testament Reference. Used when the writer refers to New Testament passages that are either fulfilled prophecy, an antitype of an Old Testament type, or a New Testament text which in some other way illuminates the passages under discussion.

Personal Application. Used when the text provides a personal or universal application of truth.

Word Picture. Indicates that the meaning of a specific word or phrase is illustrated so as to shed light on it.

INTRODUCTION

Jonah, Micah, Nahum, Habakkuk, and Zephaniah are five of twelve books in the Old Testament commonly known as the Minor Prophets. The term *Minor Prophets* is a bit of a misnomer, for neither these books nor the prophets who wrote them should be thought of in any way as minor or unimportant to the biblical story. Rather, although short in length, the messages of these prophets are a vital link in the chain of God's ongoing communication with His people.

The biblical prophets were God's spokespersons. Their job was to say exactly what God wanted to say to Israel. Their goal was to change human behavior. In order to do so, the prophets spoke about the past, the present, and the future. They sought to make God's standards for human life so relevant to the turbulent times in which they ministered that their listeners would respond and change the ways they lived. In many ways, the biblical prophets are like today's preachers, for they, too, seek to exhort God's people to live rightly.

AUTHORSHIP

Most conservative Christian and Jewish scholars hold that the men who wrote the books of the Minor Prophets were the same individuals whose names appear as the titles of the books. This is a reasonable position to hold even though the books do not explicitly state who their authors were.

The minor prophets first delivered their messages orally, as proclamations or sermons (cp. Amos 7:15; Jon. 3:4, Mic. 1:2). Eventually

Prophet

The Hebrew word which is most often translated in the Old Testament by the English word *prophet* probably meant either "one who is called" or "one who calls." Both of these ideas are illustrated in the Bible's portrayal of the prophets. The prophets were persons who were called by God, and they typically responded by calling out to the people of Israel on God's behalf (e.g., Jer. 1:4–2:2).

"All scripture is given by inspiration of God, and is profitable for doctrine, for reproof, for correction, for instruction in righteousness: That the man of God may be perfect, throughly furnished unto all good works" (2 Tim. 3:16–17, KJV).

Some Old Testament prophets seem to have held an official position in Israelite royal or temple society. Nathan (2 Sam. 12:1–15; 2 Chron. 29:25; cp. 1 Chron. 29:29), Micaiah (1 Kings 22:1–28), Isaiah (Isa. 7:3), and Hulda (2 Kings 22:12–20) had private access to the kings of Israel and Judah. Elijah did too, although he was persona non grata at the royal court (1 Kings 17:1–18:17). Jeremiah had a priestly background (Jer. 1:1), although this didn't stop him from prophesying against the Jerusalem Temple (Jer. 7:1–34; 26:1–6).

they saw to it that their messages were preserved in writing (e.g., Isa. 30:8; Jer. 29:1, 29; 30:1–2; 36:1–2, 32; Hab. 2:2). Exactly how and when this took place is difficult to say. While many questions remain, it is clear that the overall process was directed by the Holy Spirit (2 Tim. 3:16).

It is also difficult to say very much about the lives of the minor prophets. Only four of them are mentioned elsewhere in the Old Testament: Jonah (2 Kings 14:25; cp. Matt. 12:39–41; 16:1–4; Luke 11:29–32), Micah (Jer. 26:18), Haggai (Ezra 5:1; 6:14), and Zechariah (Ezra 5:1; 6:14). The rest are known only from their own books. A reasonable amount of information is given about the personal lives of Hosea (Hos. 1:1–9; 3:1–3), Amos (Amos 1:1; 7:10–15), and Jonah; but the others are almost completely unknown except for what can be inferred from their genealogy or place of birth or the overall character of their message.

A thumbnail sketch of the background of the five prophets covered in this study guide—Jonah, Micah, Nahum, Habakkuk, and Zephaniah—is provided in the table on page 3.

Until called by God, these prophets all stood in the shadow of larger world events. Although their lives may have been judged as insignificant prior to their divine call, it is clear that God spoke to them in a mighty way. Each was inspired by God's Spirit, as Micah testified of himself:

> But as for me, I am filled with power,
>   with the Spirit of the LORD,
>   and with justice and might,
> to declare to Jacob his transgression,
>   to Israel his sin (Mic. 3:8).

PROPHET	LINEAGE	HOMETOWN	TIME PERIOD OF MINISTRY
Jonah	son of Amittai	Gath-hefer, in Galilee	mid-8th century B.C.
Micah	unknown	Moresheth (Moresheth-gath), in the Judean foothills	late-8th century B.C.
Nahum	unknown	Elkosh (location unknown)	late-7th century B.C.
Habakkuk	unknown	unknown	late-7th century B.C.
Zephaniah	son of Cushi, grandson of Hezekiah (possibly the king)	unknown	late-7th century B.C.

God's true prophets could not help but speak His words (Jer. 20:9; Amos 3:3–8; cp. Acts 4:20; 1 Cor. 9:16), as even the reluctant Jonah found out (Jon. 1:1–3; 3:1–5).

DATE OF WRITING

The mid-eighth through mid-fifth centuries B.C. span the lifetimes of the "writing prophets," the men responsible for composing the books of Isaiah through Malachi. The prophets Jonah, Micah, Nahum, Habakkuk, and Zephaniah are called pre-exilic writing prophets because their books were written before Nebuchadnezzar king of Babylon destroyed Jerusalem, burned its Temple, and sent the people of Judah into Exile.

- The events of the book of Jonah took place sometime during the reign of the strongly

Prophetic activity in ancient Israel was clustered around times of crisis. Moses, the greatest prophet of the Bible, led Israel during its crucial formative years (Deut. 34:9–12). The prophet Samuel ministered to Israel as the tumultuous days of the judges gave way to the troubled monarchy of king Saul (1 Sam. 1:1–25:1; cp. 2 Chron. 35:18). Israel's greatest period of religious apostasy, in which Baal worship received official state sponsorship, was countered by the prophets Elijah and Elisha (1 Kings 17–2 Kings 13).

nationalistic Israelite king Jeroboam II, who reigned from 781 to 753 B.C. (2 Kings 14:25). During Jeroboam II's prosperous reign the feared Assyrians, who were in a temporary period of national decline, regrouped for a final series of assaults on Israel and its neighbors.

- Micah prophesied during the reigns of the Judean kings Jotham (739–731 B.C.), Ahaz (731–715 B.C.), and Hezekiah (715–686 B.C.) (Mic. 1:1; cp. Jer. 26:17–18). Micah was a contemporary of the prophet Isaiah (cp. Isa. 1:1), who also ministered in Judah and Jerusalem.

- Nahum's prophecy was directed against the nation of Assyria and its capital city, Nineveh (Nah. 1:1). Nahum mentioned the sack of No-Amon (Thebes) in Egypt, which took place in 663 B.C., and looked forward to Nineveh's destruction in 612 B.C. Hence the book of Nahum was written between these two events, probably closer to the year 612.

- Habakkuk 1:5–11 speaks of God "raising up" the Chaldeans (Babylonians), which happened just prior to the time the Assyrians fell to Babylon (612 B.C.). These verses also suggest that the Babylonians had not yet attacked Judah, which they did for the first time in 605 B.C. (cp. 2 Kings 24:7; Dan. 1:1). For these reasons, Habakkuk probably prophesied during the decade prior to 605 B.C.

- Zephaniah prophesied during the reign of the Judean king Josiah, who ruled in Jerusalem from 640 to 609 B.C. (Zech. 1:1). Many scholars date Zephaniah's prophecies to the decade preceding Josiah's sweeping religious and social reforms which took place in 621 B.C., the king's eighteenth year (cp. 2 Kings 22:3–23:25).

AUDIENCE

Bible readers do not always remember that each of the minor prophets addressed two audiences—the one that first *heard* the prophetic message as it was spoken and the one (or ones) that *read* the prophetic message once it was written down.

It is usually difficult—and in many cases impossible—to identify the exact person or persons to whom each prophetic message was first spoken. Jonah is an exception, because his messages have come down to us in the middle of a story which gives their context. In most other cases Bible readers are left to speculate. The book of Micah begins, "Hear, all you peoples" (Mic. 1:2, NKJV), but exactly who were the "peoples" that he addressed? Nahum spoke against Nineveh, but was he addressing *Ninevites* or *Israelites* as he spoke? Such questions ultimately cannot find firm answers.

One thing that is clear is that the audiences who originally heard the prophetic messages more often than not rejected them. The tone for all of the writing prophets was set at the call of Isaiah, who wrote the first and longest prophetic book in the Bible. God called Isaiah and commissioned him to tell Israel that although they would hear His messages they would not understand them because their ears, eyes, and hearts were dull and unresponsive (Isa. 6:9–10). Jeremiah, too, was rejected when he preached in the Temple and palace of Jerusalem (Jer. 7:27–28; 37:11–15; 38:6–9), as was Amos in the courts of Samaria (Amos 7:12–13). We can assume that other prophets who spoke against the people of

Some of the Old Testament prophets were favorably received by their audiences (e.g., Nathan—2 Sam. 12:1–15; Jonah—Jon. 3:3–5; Hulda—2 Kings 22:11–20), but most were not (e.g. Elijah—1 Kings 19:1–5; Micaiah—1 Kings 22:8; Elisha—2 Kings 7:1–2; Isaiah—Isa. 7:1–17; Uriah—Jer. 26:20–23; Jeremiah—37:11–15; 38:6–9). The writer of the book of Hebrews spoke of great men of faith who "quenched the violence of fire, escaped the edge of the sword, . . . had trial of mockings and scourgings, yes, and of chains and imprisonment. They were stoned, they were sawn in two, were tempted, were slain with the sword. They wandered about in sheepskins and goatskins, being destitute, afflicted, tormented" (Heb. 11:34, 36–37, NKJV). The early church fathers suggested that the writer of Hebrews had prophets such as Elijah, Elisha, Isaiah, Jeremiah, and Daniel in mind as he wrote these words.

Israel and Judah, such as Micah and Zephaniah, were also criticized for their words.

When the words of the minor prophets were written down, they were preserved in an Israelite (or Jewish) Bible. Even prophecies that were directed against foreign nations, such as Nahum's prophecy against Nineveh, were spoken to benefit God's people. The audience was as varied then as it is today. It was composed of common folk and nobles, the poor and the rich, people from the countryside and those from cities. Some believed in God while others doubted. Many questioned God's desire, willingness, or ability to be involved in the affairs of the world; others tried to use Him to further their own social, political, or religious agendas. Some read the prophets' words while trying to come to terms with what seemed to be the nonfulfillment of God's ancient promises to bless His people. These early readers were people who had entered into a covenant relationship with God, but what were they to do if the prophets were announcing that God was punishing *His own people*?

PURPOSE AND CONTENT

The biblical prophets spoke in order to call Israel and Judah back to God. Their words were rooted in the covenant which God had established with His chosen people, Israel. Over a thousand years before, God had promised that He would create a special people through Abraham and give them a special home in which to live (Gen. 12:1–3). Later, God had given Israel a set of instructions, the Torah (or Law of Moses), with which He intended to guide His people as they sought to build new lives in their new home, the Promised Land. The Torah contained a series of blessings and curses which Israel would experience as a direct result of their behavior and attitude toward God and one another (Lev. 26:1–13; Deut. 27:1–31:29). The history of ancient Israel as it appears on the pages of the Bible was a history of Israel's struggle to receive the blessings of God, all the while seeking to live without giving attention to His covenant stipulations (cp. Josh. 24:14–28; 2 Kings 17:1–23; 23:26–27).

But it was also a history in which God called Israel to return to Himself. The biblical prophets were the social and spiritual commentators of their day. Their messages were aimed at transforming God's people so that they could enjoy the blessings which God had in store for them. The prophets wanted to change the way the people of Israel thought, acted, and believed. Their goal was to bring Israel back to the kind of relationships God had intended for His people all along—relationships with Himself, between members of a family, within a workplace, and in society at large.

The prophets tried to persuade God's people to recognize that it was to their own advantage to return to God, for only by doing so would they receive His blessings. But how to persuade? Typically the prophets used a three-pronged attack: they reminded their audience of the past, they criticized their audience's present behavior, and they revealed what would happen to their audience in the future should they not change. Micah, for instance, reminded Israel of the great things that God had done for them in the past through Moses, Aaron, and Miriam (Mic. 6:3–5). He decried Israel's unjust actions in the present (Mic. 2:1–2). He warned Israel what had to happen in the near future because of their present evil behavior in the face of God's

"Persuasion was one of the key tools Old Testament prophets used to transform the way people acted. By orally communicating with their audiences, they motivated some to reconsider the way they thought about themselves, God, and their relationship with God and others. If they would transform their way of thinking (repent), God would restore His relationship with them. If the people would forsake the customs of the nations and follow God's ways, His covenant would continue."
Gary V. Smith, *The Prophets as Preachers* (Nashville: Broadman & Holman, 1994), 6.

past acts of kindness (Mic. 2:3–4). Finally, he saw a day far off when God would restore His people to the kinds of relationships which He had intended for them all along (Mic. 4:1–4).

While the biblical prophets were primarily concerned with the moral behavior of their fellow countrymen, the prophets of the ancient Near East dealt in more mundane matters. Written documents from the eighteenth century B.C. record messages of prophets who were employed by the king of Mari, a large city on the upper Euphrates River in modern Syria. Their messages offer predictions on the outcome of building projects, military campaigns, or various ritual activities, and show the prophets to have been royal "yes-men." Kings and generals in ancient Assyria and Babylon used diviners to predict the outcome of battles. These diviners used a variety of techniques to "read" the future, such as examining the entrails of a sacrificed sheep, observing the way smoke would rise, or noting the pattern of birds in flight.

Many Bible interpreters assume that the main task of the prophets was to predict the future. In fact, prediction was just one method which the prophets used to persuade their audiences to change their behavior in the present. All told, the majority of the prophetic statements in the Bible are not predictive, but exhortative. Biblical prophecy, whether foretelling (prediction) or "forth-telling" (exhortation), was primarily intended to make God's eternal standards relevant for present-day life, not to give ancient Israel—or us—a scoop on the news.

The main themes of each of the prophetic books must be read with this overarching prophetic purpose in mind.

- The book of Jonah emphasizes God's love and compassion. It was intended to remind Israel of God's all-inclusive nature and reaffirm that the covenant which He had first established with Abraham was designed to bring His blessings to all the nations of the earth (Gen. 12:1–3). In telling a twofold story of repentance (by the sailors and the Ninevites), the book teaches that God is eager to save anyone—even His own obstinate prophet.

- Micah is concerned with social justice. Because God's people had abandoned the stipulations of His covenant, society had rotted; their nation, as a result, would fall. Yet hope remained in Temple worship—the current focal point of God's activity on earth—and in the Messiah who would one day set all Israel aright.

- The book of Nahum was written to teach that God eventually does punish sin—personal sin, corporate sin, and national sin. Although the prophecies of Nahum were written about Nineveh, they were addressed with Israel in mind and served as a warning of what could well happen to God's people should they continue to act just like the nations around them.

- The book of Habakkuk wrestles with what sometimes seems like God's inactivity in the face of chaos. God's people are called to be faithful, to wait, and to hope in Him. Habakkuk boldly declared that in the end God would triumph over evil.

- The book of Zephaniah also addresses the inactivity of God. Zephaniah's contribution to this dilemma is far-reaching. A day was coming, Zephaniah declared, when God would overturn the world and set everything aright. He called this day "the day of the Lord."

Together, these five prophets challenged Israel and Judah to change both their behavior and their ways of thinking. They spoke of judgment, but they also held out a glorious hope for anyone who repented and turned to God.

LITERARY STYLE AND THEMATIC STRUCTURE

While the various books of the Minor Prophets may at first glance seem repetitious and perhaps disjointed or confusing, each, in fact, is a unique and well-crafted work of art with a distinctive character and shape.

The various sayings of the biblical prophets are described by several different Hebrew words or phrases, the most common of which appear in English as "the word of the Lord," "[thus] says the Lord" and "the burden." The phrases "the word of the Lord" (e.g. Jon. 1:1; Mic. 1:1; Zech. 1:1) and "[thus] says the Lord" (e.g. Mic. 4:6; Zeph. 1:2–3) indicate what God says, and communicate that what was spoken by the prophets is a reflection of God's very character or essence. The descriptive word *burden* introduces a prophetic message that is threatening or judgmental in character and hence was difficult for the prophet to deliver and for the people to accept (e.g. Nah. 1:1; Hab. 1:1).

Each of the books of the Minor Prophets begins with a statement describing the kind of message it contains. For Jonah, Micah, and Zephaniah, the prophetic message was a "word of the Lord" (Jon. 1:1; Mic. 1:1; Zeph. 1:1), while for Nahum and Habakkuk it was a "burden," so named because it was difficult to bear (Nah. 1:1; Hab. 1:1). Within these broad prophetic contexts the prophets used various literary forms, including laments (Mic. 1:8–16; 7:1–6), hymns (Jon. 2:2–9; Nah. 1:2–8; Hab. 3:1–19), taunt songs (Nah. 2:11–13; 3:14–17; Hab. 2:6–19), judgment oracles (Zeph. 1:2–6), woe oracles (Mic. 2:1–11; Nah. 3:1–7; Zeph. 3:1–8), salvation oracles (Zeph. 3:9–20), and a covenant lawsuit (Mic. 6:1–16). Many of these forms were borrowed from the broader literary and oral culture in which the prophets lived. Understanding them helps us to interpret the Bible's prophetic message.

Prophetic sayings were usually spoken—and recorded—in poetry (e.g. Mic. 1–7; Nah. 1–3; Hab. 1–3; Zeph. 1–3). Poetry is a particularly valuable means of prophetic expression; for by using vivid images, riveting sound patterns, and otherwise "heightened" speech, the prophet enabled God's words to penetrate directly into the human soul.

Less frequently the biblical prophets wrote in prose. When they did so, they sometimes told a story by using third-person narrative. The best example is the book of Jonah, a beautiful short story which packs a powerful prophetic punch. Other books of the Minor Prophets such as Amos (Amos 7:10, 12–15) and Haggai also contain narrative elements, but none tells a complete story like Jonah (cp. also Isa. 7:1–17; 36:1–39:8; Jer. 36:1–45:5; 52:1–34; Dan. 1:1–6:28).

The biblical prophets chose the literary styles that were most appropriate to convey their divine messages. In each case thematic and literary elements were combined in unique ways to form the prophetic book's structure. The basic structural outline for each book is as follows:

Jonah:

>An encounter with some sailors (Jon. 1)
>An encounter with God (Jon. 2)
>An encounter with the Ninevites (Jon. 3)
>An encounter with God (Jon. 4)

Micah:

>Judgment and hope for God's people (Mic. 1–2)
>Judgment and hope for God's leaders (Mic. 3–5)
>Judgment and hope for God's people (Mic. 6–7)

Nahum:

>The doom of Nineveh (Nah. 1)
>The siege and fall of Nineveh (Nah. 2–3)

Habakkuk:

>A discourse with God about injustice in Judah (Hab. 1:1–11)
>A discourse with God about injustice against Judah (Hab. 1:12–2:20)
>A prayer of reconciliation (Hab. 3:1–19)

Zephaniah:

>The day of the Lord as a day of judgment (Zeph. 1:1–3:8)
>The day of the Lord as a day of hope (Zeph. 3:9–20)

In Middle Eastern culture generally—in the past as well as today—speech in a formal setting is often poetic. Poetry is an educated and artful way of speaking and signifies that the communication is of great importance and should not be taken lightly. In this light it is appropriate that when God speaks in the Bible His words usually are poetic in character.

PRINCIPLES FOR INTERPRETATION

Biblical prophecy ought not to be approached casually, as if the first impression that jumps off the page must be the correct one. The interpreter's job can be made easier and more enjoyable—and the results more accurate—if he or she keeps in mind some basic principles of interpretation:

- Every prophecy has a historical context that governs its meaning. This context includes the political, social, and spiritual background of the prophecy; the nature of the prophet's original audience(s); and the reason this original audience needed to hear the prophetic message. It should be assumed that every prophetic utterance made sense within its original historical context.

- Every prophecy has a theological (or biblical) context that governs its meaning. Each verse of prophecy must be read with the verses on either side of it in mind and in light of the overall message of the book in which it is found. Furthermore, because each biblical prophecy supplemented previously given biblical revelation, it is important to know earlier portions of the Bible and to strive to understand how the prophet interacted with what God had already said. It should be assumed that every prophetic passage makes sense within its overall biblical context.

- An interpreter must know what a prophetic text meant "back then" before trying to determine how it applies "right now."

- Prediction may be conditional. This Jonah found out when God spared Nineveh in spite of his own prophetic word of judgment.

- When the prophets spoke of the future, they seldom gave exact time references. Sometimes their prophecies were fulfilled in a relatively short period of time; others are prophecies yet to be fulfilled.

- Most biblical prophecy was spoken and written in poetry, and poetry almost always has a figurative aspect. Sometimes poetic figures are easy to understand, while other times they are rather difficult. An interpreter must become sensitive to figurative language and learn to use a prophecy's historical and theological contexts to discern what each poetic figure means.

- Keeping an eye on the New Testament will help Bible readers interpret some Old Testament prophecies. Many prophecies, of course, speak about Jesus the Messiah. A New Testament fulfillment of a prophecy must not violate that prophecy's original Old Testament context. Keeping this in mind will help an interpreter decide whether a predictive prophecy has a single or a double fulfillment or whether its fulfillment should be seen in terms of a process.

- Finally, with the insight of the Holy Spirit, an interpreter must let the text speak for itself. A commonsense approach often makes a lot of sense in biblical interpretation.

It must not be thought that learning to read the biblical prophets is too daunting a task or that everything must be known before anything can be known. Rather, it is helpful to keep in mind the words of Thomas à Kempis: "Our own curiosity often hinders us in reading the Scriptures, when we examine and discuss that which we should pass over without more ado. If you desire to reap profit, read with humility, simplicity and faithfulness" (*Of the Imitation of Christ*, 1, v. 2).

In addition to these general rules of interpretation, it is important that all readers of biblical prophecy understand the basic nature of biblical poetry.

Biblical poetry, like ancient Canaanite poetry, was composed in units of two, three, or four parallel lines. Within these units each individual line in some way repeated yet built on the thought of the previous line. This "rhyming of thought" typically is classified into three types:

Synonymous parallelism, in which the second or subsequent line repeats or reinforces the previous line. This occurs twice in Micah 2:12 (NKJV):

- I will surely assemble all of you, O Jacob,
- I will surely gather the remnant of Israel;
- I will put them together like sheep of the fold,
- Like a flock in the midst of their pasture.

Antithetical parallelism, in which the second or subsequent line contrasts or negates the previous line, as in Micah 3:4 (NKJV):

- Then they will cry to the LORD,
- But he will not hear them.

Synthetic (climactic or "stair step") parallelism, in which the second or subsequent line adds to the thought of the first line, as in Micah 2:13 (NKJV):

- The one who breaks open will come up before them;
- They will break out, pass through the gate, and go out by it;
- Their king will pass before them, with the LORD at their head.

By keeping these rules of interpretation in mind, it will become possible to read, enjoy, and profit from the Bible's prophetic books.

THEOLOGY

The Minor Prophets are theologically rich books that can be appreciated only by carefully reading (and rereading) them, first in the context of the Old Testament and then in light of the New Testament. Many foundational biblical truths are proclaimed in the books of Jonah, Micah, Nahum, Habakkuk, and Zephaniah, such as:

- God is sovereign over all people and all nations (Jon. 4:6–11; Mic. 4:11–13; Nah. 1:3–8; Hab. 1:5–6; 3:2; Zeph. 2:1–15).

- God can be trusted to do what is good and right (Nah. 1:7–8; Hab. 1:1–5; Zeph. 3:5).

- God keeps His promises (Hab. 2:1–3).

- God expects His people to remain faithful to Him (Mic. 3:1, 5, 9; 6:1–16; Hab. 2:4; Zeph. 2:3).

- Judgment is inescapable for those who turn against God (Mic. 1:2–9; Nah. 1:2–3, 9; Zeph. 1:2–6).

- God is continually gracious to His people and wants to restore them to favor (Jon. 4:6–11; Mic. 2:12–13; 4:1–8; 5:7–9; 7:18–20; Nah. 1:15; 2:2; Hab. 3:17–19; Zeph. 3:9–10, 14–20).

- God's plan for the world included a coming Messiah who would restore God's people to Him (Mic. 2:12–13; 5:2–4).

A covenant is a compact between two parties mutually binding them to certain agreed-upon obligations and benefits. Scripture refers to a number of covenants drawn up between various persons or nations. Covenants instituted by God include those made with Noah (Gen. 9:8–17), Abraham (Gen. 15:17–21; 17:2, 9–14), Moses (Exod. 19:5–6), and David (2 Sam. 7:12–16; cp. 23:5), and the New Covenant of Jeremiah (Jer. 31:31–34). Although the form and details of these covenants differed, their basic content remained the same: I will be your God, you will be My people, and I will dwell in your midst (cp. Gen. 17:7; Exod. 6:6–7; 19:4–6).

The theological message of the Bible's prophetic books is grounded in God's covenant of promise. The covenant which God had established with the children of Israel at Mount Sinai bound Him and His people together in a close relationship (Exod. 19:5–6). Israel was chosen by God to live in a land which He had specially prepared for them. His people were expected to remain faithful to Him. If they failed to do so, they would not only cease to be prosperous and successful, but they would also be driven from their land. If they returned to Him, God would restore their fortunes and pour out His blessings upon them.

This message is also the underlying theme of the books of Joshua, Judges, 1 and 2 Samuel, and 1 and 2 Kings. It is largely for this reason that in Jewish tradition these books of history are called the "Former Prophets," while the books of Isaiah through Malachi (with the exception of Daniel and Lamentations) are designated the "Latter Prophets." In broad outline both tell the same story, although the books of history present a more politically-oriented account of ancient Israel's history while the books of prophecy offer a more intimate look into everyday life.

THE MEANING OF THE PROPHETS FOR TODAY

The books of the Minor Prophets continue to hold meaning for Christians today even though they were written halfway around the world and more than twenty-five hundred years ago. Because "all Scripture is useful" for Christians (2 Tim. 3:16), it is important that believers strive to understand not just what these books say but also what they say *for us*.

The biblical prophets spoke to specific audiences, but their messages were fueled by timeless themes and eternal truths. God continues to love His people and guide their lives for His glory. He continues to bless those who choose to believe in Him. Because He is sovereign in history, we can be sure that He is in control of the many circumstances of our lives. Because God kept His promises to Israel, we know that He will also keep His promises to us. Because God expected Israel to be faithful to His covenant, He expects us to be faithful to Him as well. Israel was held accountable for behavior that was self-centered, impure, and violent, and so are we. If the nations of Israel and Judah could decay from within and fall apart—indeed, if mighty Nineveh could come to naught, then our nations, notwithstanding their might and godly heritage, can do the same.

The books of the Minor Prophets are also relevant for Christians because they look forward to a day of redemption. The prophets spoke of a coming One who would solve the problems of a sinful world. Some of their prophecies spoke of His first coming, and others looked to a far-off day when all peoples would be subject to His rule.

Finally, the minor prophets provide models for effective communication in the church. Today the role of God's spokespersons is found primarily in preachers. It is they who forcefully, audibly, and publicly bring God's truths to bear on the spiritual and social ills of society. By studying the various preaching techniques of the biblical prophets, preachers can learn how to prompt change more effectively in the hearts of their listeners.

The biblical prophets sought to bring God down to earth so that we can be raised up to God. John Stott has written that God did the same in Christ. "God condescended to our humanity, though without surrendering His deity. [As preachers], our bridges too must be firmly anchored on both sides of the chasm, by refusing either to compromise the divine content of the message or to ignore the human context in which it has to be spoken. We have to plunge fearlessly into both worlds, ancient and modern, biblical and contemporary, and to listen attentively to both. For only then shall we understand what each is saying, and so discern the Spirit's message to the present generation." John R. W. Stott, *Between Two Worlds: The Art of Preaching in the Twentieth Century* (Eerdmans, 1982), 145.

STUDY OUTLINE

I. Jonah's First Response to God's Call
   (1:1–2:10)
   A. An Encounter with Some Sailors
      (1:1–16)
      1. Big Steps in the Wrong Direction
         (vv. 1–3)
      2. A Desperate Dialogue (vv. 4–16)
   B. An Encounter with God (1:17–2:10)
II. Jonah's Second Response to God's Call
   (3:1–4:11)
   A. An Encounter with the Ninevites
      (3:1–10)
      1. Small Steps in the Right Direction
         (vv. 1–3)
      2. Two Desperate Declarations
         (vv. 4–10)
   B. An Encounter with God (4:1–11)

Although only forty-eight verses long, the book of Jonah is packed with spiritual truths. Among the major themes found in the book are:

- *The sovereignty of God.* By working out His plans in spite of Jonah's failures, God shows Himself to be the sovereign Lord of history.
- *Mercy and grace.* God is compassionate to whomever He wants to be.
- *Responsibility.* Simple head knowledge of God is insufficient. All who are given a task by God have a responsibility to perform that task to the best of their ability and devotion.
- *Servanthood.* By disobeying God's call, Jonah provides a negative example of servanthood.

- *Repentance.* God's prophets did not simply hawk divine judgment but spoke to encourage people to repent.
- *Missions.* God wants to reach out to people everywhere. Human narrow-mindedness, bigotry, and apathy will not stand in His way.

JONAH'S FIRST RESPONSE TO GOD'S CALL (1:1–2:10)

The story of Jonah is told in four short episodes. In the first two (ch. 1–2), Jonah encountered a shipload of pagan sailors and then met God in a most awkward place. From the outset it is clear that he had lived *among* God's people for so long that he had forgotten what it was to be a part *of* God's people.

An Encounter with Some Sailors (1:1–16)

God called Jonah to go to Nineveh, but Jonah instead fled in the opposite direction. God used Jonah to convert a shipload of pagan sailors anyway.

Big Steps in the Wrong Direction (vv. 1–3)

The book of Jonah opens with God's call to speak out against human wickedness (1:1–2). God told Jonah to cry out against Nineveh, the mighty Assyrian city, because, like Sodom and Gomorrah of old, its wickedness could no longer be overlooked (cp. Gen. 18:20; 19:1–29). Jonah was not told what, specifically, to preach, although most interpreters assume that it was to be a message of judgment.

Dutifully Jonah arose as he was commanded but turned and fled in the opposite direction, to Joppa and then toward Tarshish. Tarshish was a distant port probably located in Spain. It was as far away from landlocked Nineveh as Jonah could get.

"For God so loved the world that He gave His only begotten Son, that whoever believes in Him should not perish but have everlasting life" (John 3:16, NKJV).

According to 2 Kings 14:25, Jonah the son of Amittai (1:1) was both a "servant" and a "prophet" of God who ministered during the reign of Jeroboam king of Israel. This Jeroboam, the second of Israel's kings with that name (2 Kings 14:23–29; cp. 1 Kings 12:25–14:20), reigned from 781 to 753 B.C. During his reign ancient Israel experienced a time of political and economic revival as the fortunes of the once mighty Assyrian Empire declined. Jeroboam was able to expand Israel's borders "from the entrance of Hamath" (in modern northern Syria) "to the Sea of the Arabah" (the Dead Sea). Israel's northern border thus extended as far as it had been under Solomon (cp. 1 Kings 8:65).

Nineveh, located above the upper Tigris River, was some five hundred miles northeast of Jonah's hometown, Gath-hepher in Galilee (cp. 2 Kings 14:25). Joppa, the Mediterranean port to which he fled, lay to the southwest. The ruins of ancient Nineveh are near modern Mosul in Iraq, while ancient Joppa lies within the Israeli city of Tel Aviv.

Throughout the biblical story God typically called His servants to "Arise!" (cp. Gen. 13:17; 35:1; Deut. 9:12; Josh. 1:2; 1 Sam. 16:12; Jer. 1:17; Ezek. 3:22; Matt. 2:20; Acts 8:26, etc.). God also called Jonah to "arise," leading us as readers to expect only the best from him. Instead Jonah "went down," first to Joppa and then onto a ship heading west (1:3). By arising to "go down," Jonah not only disobeyed God but also sought to renounce his divine call.

The reason for Jonah's flight—away from Nineveh but also away from the Lord—is not given in chapter 1. Jonah wrestled with his divine call, and we are left to struggle with his motives and actions. By not providing all of the answers to Jonah's behavior, the writer of the book of Jonah sought to involve us in his story. We are left to try to fill in the blanks. Eventually we must answer the final question that God posed to Jonah, a question that ends the book (4:11). By doing so, we are compelled to identify with the reluctant prophet and even see ourselves in him.

"Where can I go from Your Spirit? Or where can I flee from Your presence? . . . If I take the wings of the morning, and dwell in the uttermost parts of the sea, even there Your hand shall lead me, and Your right hand shall hold me" (Ps. 139:7, 9–10, NKJV).

■ *Jonah, God's servant and prophet, renounced*
■ *his divine call and fled. This was tantamount*
■ *to open rebellion against God. Would such*
■ *blatant rebellion be punished, or would God*
■ *be patient with His recalcitrant prophet?*

A Desperate Dialogue (vv. 4–16)

Jonah ran from God but could not hide. He thought that he could get away from God simply by leaving the land of Israel. His thoughts were consistent with the prevailing pagan theology of the day: each nation's god was thought to be powerless outside of his or her own land (cp. 1 Kings 20:23; 2 Kings 18:33–35). The Phoenician sailors with whom Jonah sailed no doubt believed this (1:5–6). They were the heirs of the ancient Canaanite religious system which so much of the Old Testament speaks against. By taking refuge among Phoenician sailors, Jonah implicitly declared that, at least for the moment, he preferred the Canaanite way of life to that of Israel.

God intervened by sending (lit. "hurling") a great storm upon the sea, threatening to sink the ship (v. 4). The sailors, distraught, immediately turned to their gods for help, but Jonah "went down" again, this time into the very bottom of the ship to fall asleep (v. 5). The ship's captain confronted Jonah, who appeared not to appreciate the seriousness of the situation, but Jonah didn't reply (v. 6). The contrast is striking: the pagan sailors, without knowledge of the Lord God, were sensitive to the world of the divine, while Jonah, God's true prophet, not only shut himself off from God but was also totally inattentive to the life-and-death needs of other people.

The sailors cast lots to see if the storm had been caused by the actions of one of the passengers on board (v. 7). The lot fell to Jonah, who, when pressed, finally admitted that he "feared the LORD," the true God who had made the very sea that was threatening to kill them all (vv. 8–9, NKJV). Jonah spoke well, but his hesitancy to act suggests that he really didn't believe what he was saying. The sailors "were terrified," now knowing the name of the God in whose hands their lives lay (v. 10).

The nationality of the sailors is not given, but they must have been Phoenicians. The Phoenicians controlled the shipping lanes of the Mediterranean during the time of the Israelite monarchy (cp. Ezek. 27:1–36). They lived along the rocky Mediterranean coast north of Israel in modern Lebanon. The major Phoenician cities were Tyre and Sidon. Hiram king of Tyre supplied timber from the mountains of Lebanon for Solomon's Temple (1 Kings 5:1–12). Jesus visited Tyre and Sidon where He healed the daughter of a Gentile woman (Mark 7:24–30).

Twice Jesus stilled storms on the Sea of Galilee that threatened to drown His disciples. Once, like Jonah, He slept in the boat while the storm raged around Him (Matt. 8:23–27). Another time Jesus walked to the boat on top of the water in the midst of a storm (Matt. 14:22–33).

In the ancient Near East, casting lots was an accepted means of determining the will of the gods, or, in the case of the sailors with whom Jonah was sailing, finding out who had offended the gods. Unlike other forms of divination, casting lots was not a forbidden practice in ancient Israel (cp. Deut. 18:9–14). The Old Testament makes numerous references to decisions determined by casting lots (e.g., Lev. 16:7–10; Num. 26:55; Josh. 14:2; Neh. 10:34; Esther 3:7). The Urim and Thummim were a form of lots by which God's will was determined (Exod. 28:30). The apostles used lots to choose Judas' successor (Acts 1:26). According to Proverbs 16:33, "The lot is cast into the lap, But its every decision is from the LORD" (NKJV).

Jonah insisted that he be thrown overboard to calm the storm (vv. 11–12). His motives are unclear: did he want to appease God through self-sacrifice, did he want to die and thereby end his flight from God, or was he starting to own up to his responsibilities? Regardless of his motives, the sailors sought to save *his* life (as well as theirs) and rowed for shore (v. 13), but in the end capitulated to Jonah's request. Calling on the Lord—the God of whom Jonah had reluctantly spoken—for mercy in the face of murder, they threw Jonah to the wind and waves (vv. 14–15). The sea became still, and the pagan sailors, awestruck by the power of the true God, "feared the Lord exceedingly, offered a sacrifice to the LORD and made vows" (v. 16, NKJV).

Throughout the storm, the pagan sailors showed more spiritual and basic human sensitivity than did Jonah, the chosen prophet schooled in the ways of God. In the end they did all of the things that true Israelite believers were supposed to, while Jonah, for all his privilege and position, was as good as dead.

- Jonah, in spite of himself, was able to bring
- the saving message of the Lord God to a
- pagan world. He almost paid with his life for
- his obstinacy. People were saved—physi-
- cally and spiritually—but only because of
- the direct hand of God in human affairs.

An Encounter with God (1:17–2:10)

God rescued Jonah by appointing a large fish to swallow him before he drowned in the crashing sea (1:17). It is not possible to identify this fish with a known species of whale or other large sea creature. Jonah spent three days and nights in the fish's belly before being vomited onto dry land (2:10). That he survived the experience can only be understood as a miracle.

Jonah prayed to God while he was in the belly of the fish. His prayer, in poetry, was a short psalm of thanksgiving. Its tone is unexpected given Jonah's situation, for it speaks of past deliverance as if Jonah's troubles were already over, rather than voicing a cry in the midst of trouble.

Jonah's prayer follows the pattern of other prayers of thanksgiving found in the book of Psalms (e.g. 116; 118; 138). Typically such psalms contain a vivid description of trouble followed by a promise to serve God by sacrificing to Him or paying vows. Jonah's prayer is also reminiscent of the psalms because almost everything that he said is found—although expressed slightly differently—somewhere in the book of Psalms (v. 2—Pss. 18:4–6; 118:5; 120:1; 130:1; v. 3—Pss. 42:7; 88:6–7; v. 4—Ps. 31:22; v. 5—Ps. 69:1; v. 7—Ps. 18:6; v. 8—Ps. 31:6; v. 9—Pss. 3:8; 50:14).

Jonah began his prayer by comparing his descent into the sea to a drowning man. As he sank, he passed billowing waves (2:3) and choking seaweed (2:5) before settling down beside the "roots of the mountains" (2:6). Jonah arrived at a "land whose bars closed upon me forever" (2:6, RSV), a common poetic figure in the ancient Near East for the abode of the dead. To reinforce his hopeless fate, Jonah lamented that he was in "the belly of Sheol" (2:2) and "the pit" (2:6, NKJV). Having "gone down" as far as he could, he was, in his estimation, finally out of

"The belly of the fish is not a happy place to live, but it is a good place to learn." Learning can often be difficult. Our own experiences are sometimes uncomfortable and leave us scarred, as the gastrointestinal juices mixed with bits of seaweed and odd critters did to Jonah.

The scribes and Pharisees demanded a sign from Jesus to prove that His authority was from God. Jesus offered no sign except "the sign of the prophet Jonah. For as Jonah was three days and nights in the belly of the great fish, so will the Son of Man be three days and three nights in the heart of the earth" (Matt. 12:39–40, NKJV; cp. 16:4; Luke 11:29–32). Jonah served as a sign to the Ninevites in that he appeared to them as one who had been delivered from certain death. In the same way, Jesus overcame death to offer salvation to "an evil and adulterous generation" (Matt. 12:39).

Sheol

The Hebrew word *Sheol* is difficult to translate. The origin of the word is unclear. Depending on the context, Sheol can mean "death," "the grave," "hell," or simply "the afterlife." The Greek translation of the Old Testament (the Septuagint) and the New Testament translate the word *Sheol* by the Greek word *Hades*.

"Repentance always brings a person to the point of saying, 'I have sinned.' The surest sign that God is at work in his life is when he says that and means it. Anything less is simply sorrow for having made foolish mistakes." Oswald Chambers, *My Utmost for His Highest,* (Oswald Chambers Publications Association Ltd., 7 Dec. 1992)

God's reach—and, for all intents and purposes, as good as dead.

Yet Jonah spoke of hope. At first he despaired, noting that he would never again see God's Temple (2:4). But when Jonah remembered God, his spirits revived (2:7). He looked forward to visiting the Temple some day, there offering sacrifices to God and fulfilling the vows he had made (2:8–9). Jonah claimed that he was not, after all, like the pagans who "forsake their true loyalty" (2:8, RSV), a reference to unbelievers who do not follow the ways of the Lord God.

What are we to make of Jonah's prayer? On one hand his words are a beautiful study of devotion and provide triumphant hope for all who need deliverance. On the other hand, they don't quite fit the events which are described in Jonah 1.

Having fled from God, Jonah needed to repent. We might expect him to pray a sinner's prayer, much as David did following his sin with Bathsheba (Ps. 51; cp. 2 Sam. 11:1–12:23). Instead, without a word of repentance, he recounted how God delivered him from drowning and then voiced his thankful response to *that*. As readers, we are left with the impression that Jonah almost expected to be delivered; he was, after all, God's chosen prophet.

Without a clear statement of repentance, it is difficult to know the attitude behind Jonah's prayer. Bible interpreters are divided on their assessment of it. Jonah claimed that God cast him into the sea (2:3), but it was Jonah himself who had asked to be thrown overboard, and that as he was running away from God (1:12, 15). Does Jonah see God's sovereign hand in his own foolish actions, or is he just reciting phrases from the Psalms, "quoting Bible verses" as it were, to justify his privileged position as a prophet? Jonah promised to sacrifice and fulfill his vows as a good Israelite and not be like the pagans who worship idols (2:8–9), all the while oblivious to the fact that the sailors had already done just that (cp. 1:16). Was Jonah's faith genuine like the pagans onboard ship, or was he simply saying what he thought God wanted to hear? What is clear is that, even if Jonah *did* repent in chapter 2, his actions in the rest of the book show him not really to have understood what repentance means.

"And if we obey God, we must disobey ourselves, and it is this disobeying ourselves wherein the hardness of obeying God consists."
From the sermon of Father Mapple in Herman Melville's *Moby Dick*.

■ *God turned Jonah around, and the trip back*
■ *to dry land was anything but pleasant. Jonah*
■ *spoke well of God while still in the fish. His*
■ *response once back on land would determine*
■ *whether he had truly come to his senses.*

QUESTIONS TO GUIDE YOUR STUDY

1. What part of Jonah's culture and heritage might have caused him to begrudge God's love for others? What causes us to do the same?

2. How would you characterize Jonah's prayer in chapter 2? Was Jonah sincere? naive? desperate? grateful? repentant?

3. How typical are Jonah's actions and attitudes for preachers and missionaries, today's spokespersons for God?

JONAH'S SECOND RESPONSE TO GOD'S CALL (3:1–4:11)

The last two episodes of the book of Jonah (ch. 3–4) recount what happened when Jonah finally went to Nineveh. The focus is not on the salvation of Nineveh—a momentous event in its

Nineveh is described as "an exceedingly great city, a three-day journey in extent" (3:3, NKJV). This phrase is difficult in Hebrew, and more so because the walled city of Nineveh uncovered by archaeologists is only eight miles in circumference. It probably indicates either that the journey around the larger administrative district of Nineveh took three days or that Jonah spent three days preaching up and down the streets of the city.

own right—but on Jonah's response to the sovereignty to God.

An Encounter with the Ninevites (3:1–10)

The wicked city of Nineveh turned to God in the face of impending judgment. God spared the city, just as He had the sailors in chapter 1.

Small Steps in the Right Direction (vv. 1–3)
Again God called Jonah to go to Nineveh (v. 1). This time God didn't tell him to cry out *against* the city in judgment but to "preach *to* it the message that I tell you" (v. 2, NKJV). The change is significant, for it indicates that now God was allowing Nineveh room to repent. By now Jonah knew personally that God's mercy and compassion were greater than human propensity for evil. Later Jonah would reveal that he didn't want to give Nineveh a chance to repent because he knew that God would probably spare the city, which was something he didn't want done (cp. 4:2). Nevertheless Jonah arose and went anyway, now knowing that it was pointless to run away.

Jonah obeyed God's second call. How willing he was to go is a matter of interpretation. Most assume Jonah's willingness, reasoning that anyone who repents responds by following God. On the other hand, if Jonah truly *had* repented, he needn't have waited for a second call before going on to Nineveh, something he should have done in the first place.

ℵ

- *Jonah finally made it to Nineveh. God gave*
- *him a second chance whether he wanted one*
- *or not. In this God showed that Jonah, in*
- *spite of his past blunders and obstinacy, still*
- *had value for the kingdom of God.*

Two Desperate Declarations (vv. 4–10)

Abraham had pled fervently on behalf of the cities of Sodom and Gomorrah when God told him that they were about to be destroyed (Gen. 18:16–33). He knew that the cities were wicked but wanted them to be spared for the sake of a few righteous persons who might still live there. Jonah, apparently, had no such compulsions. Whether his message "Forty more days and Nineveh will be overturned" (v. 4) was what God had indeed told him to say, or whether God's message to Jonah included the hope of divine forbearance, the text does not say. In any case Jonah was unwilling, or unable, to hold out the same chance of repentance for Nineveh that God had offered to him while at sea.

The people of Nineveh heard Jonah's brief sermon as a desperate cry of judgment, and they responded favorably. All of them, "from the greatest to the least," believed in God, then backed up their belief by action (v. 5). By fasting and wearing sackcloth—traditional signs of mourning, the people of Nineveh threw themselves on the mercy of the God revealed by Jonah. Like the pagan sailors of Jonah 1, the people of Nineveh turned to God after His prophet had spoken only a few words. In neither case should the credit for their spiritual awakening be given to Jonah.

The ruins of Nineveh were first excavated in 1847 and have been the focus of archaeological work on and off ever since. The remains of marvelous structures have been uncovered, including massive temples to the gods Nabu and Ishtar and ornate palaces of the Assyrian kings. Intricate reliefs showing battle scenes and daily life in ancient Assyria lined the walls of the royal palaces during Nineveh's heyday, the time of the late Israelite monarchy. Nineveh attained its greatest splendor in the century following Jonah's visit. During that time the Assyrian king Sennacherib (cp. 2 Kings 18:13) made the city his capital and furnished it with public gardens and an aqueduct system that brought water into the city from the eastern mountains.

There are no historical records from ancient Assyria attesting to Jonah's message or the religious revival which swept through Nineveh in his day. Some conclude that this proves the event never took place. But the Assyrians typically recorded only events which cast their nation in a positive light.

Jesus used the repentance of Nineveh as an example of what the scribes and Pharisees were not doing (Matt. 12:41; Luke 11:29–32). Like Jonah, the scribes and Pharisees knew all about God's requirements, but such head knowledge failed to trickle down to their hearts.

Eventually the king of Nineveh also heard the message of judgment, possibly from Jonah but more probably from his own subjects (v. 6). He, too, sat in sackcloth and ashes and made an official decree that his entire kingdom repent before God (vv. 7–8). He hoped that God would spare his city (v. 9). All in all, the king's desperate decree contained far more gospel than Jonah's brief call for judgment.

The sailors and their captain, the Ninevites and their king were all pagans; yet each did something Jonah himself is never specifically said to have done: they repented in humility before God. All held out hope that God might be merciful (1:6, 14; 3:9), but Jonah himself saw no reason to voice the same even though he knew in his heart that God would probably spare Nineveh (cp. 4:2).

God responded to the attitude and actions of the Ninevites and spared their city from destruction (v. 10). Jonah's prophecy did not come true, but this does not make it false (cp. Deut. 18:15–22). Most biblical prophecies, whether they spoke of coming judgment or future blessing, had a built-in conditional aspect. Such prophecies were meant to change the behavior of the audience to which they were spoken so that judgment would no longer be necessary. Often, however—as it was in the case of Nineveh—repentance was only temporary; and the judgment, postponed, eventually fell (cp. Nahum).

ℕ

- *Jonah preached to Nineveh, and the city*
- *repented before God. God spared the city,*
- *showing that His mercy triumphs over*
- *judgment.*

An Encounter with God (4:1–11)

Jonah became very angry with God when he saw that Nineveh was not going to be destroyed (v. 1). He told God that he had suspected Nineveh would be saved from destruction all along and preferred to die rather than be the instrument through which Israel's chief enemy was spared (vv. 2–3).

Jonah had his theology right: God *was* "gracious and merciful . . ., slow to anger and abundant in lovingkindness, One who relents from doing harm" (v. 2, NKJV). In saying so, Jonah quoted words Moses had spoken to God (cp. Exod. 34:6), much as he had already replayed statements from the Psalms in his prayer in chapter 2. Jonah knew God's character all along—when he ran to Tarshish and while he sat, indignant, at the outskirts of Nineveh (cp. 4:5). He was, in fact, still running from God, an indication that his prayer in the belly of the fish had not reached into his own heart and soul.

Jonah could not comprehend God's actions, believing instead that divine mercy should extend only to Israel (cp. Exod. 34:6–7; Ps. 86:15). He preferred that God destroy Israel's chief enemy, an enemy whom, he correctly surmised, would one day arise to capture and burn his own homeland (cp. 2 Kings 17:1–6). God's justice (the Ninevites deserved to die) did not fit, in Jonah's mind, with divine compassion.

"If my people who are called by my name humble themselves, and pray and seek my face, and turn from their wicked ways, then I will hear from heaven, and will forgive their sin and heal their land" (2 Chron. 7:14, RSV).

The note in 2 Kings 14:25 that Jeroboam, the king of Israel, expanded the borders of his kingdom to the extent that they were in the days of Solomon has a strongly nationalistic flavor. Israel grew strong militarily under the leadership of Jeroboam, a king who did not follow the ways of God (cp. 2 Kings 14:23–24). It is significant that it was Jonah who prophesied that Jeroboam would be successful. Jonah seems to have been a prophet who wanted above all for his nation to succeed politically and militarily.

Jonah's hometown, Gath-hepher in Galilee, was only three miles from Nazareth. Growing up in Nazareth, Jesus must have known that Jonah hailed from the same area and no doubt reflected on the prophet's ministry. Both Jonah and Jesus preached that God's plan of salvation included the Gentiles. But both ministered among a people who believed that God was interested only in the Jews (or the Israelites). On one occasion, after Nicodemus had defended Jesus' authority, the chief priests and Pharisees chided, "Are you from Galilee too? Search and you will see that no prophet is to rise from Galilee" (John 7:52, RSV). They had overlooked—conveniently for their cause, which was focused exclusively on the Jews—that Jonah, too, was a Galilean.

Jonah had forgotten—or never quite realized—that he, too, was already the unworthy object of God's mercy (1:3, 17; 2:10).

Questioned by God for his anger, Jonah retreated a safe distance from Nineveh to wait for the fire and brimstone which he still hoped must come (vv. 4–5). He built a small hut for shade; the Hebrew term, *sukka*, suggests a flimsy structure made of leafy branches that would quickly wither in the heat (cp. Lev. 23:41–43). With Jonah's own effort to gain relief from the burning sun inadequate, God prepared a special plant for shade (v. 8).

Jonah was very pleased with the plant for which he could claim no credit but again wished to die when God caused the plant to be devoured and a "vehement east wind"—a *hamsin*—nearly sapped his life from him (vv. 7–8, NKJV). Again God questioned Jonah's anger, this time about the plant. Jonah could see no further than his own discomfort; he became so despondent that he preferred death even to getting up to find shade elsewhere (v. 9).

God then drove to the point. Jonah had been upset over something as insignificant as a single plant; should not he also be concerned over the eternal destiny of 120,000 people who, without knowledge of God, "cannot discern between their right hand and their left?" (v. 11, NKJV). Jonah's priorities were tragically wrong. The object lesson pointed to God's love and compassion for everyone.

The book of Jonah ends with God's third question of the chapter. Jonah's answer is not given, although it is predictable in light of the bitterness of his previous answers (cp. 4:4, 9). In the end the prophet apparently still ran from God, not yet wanting (or able) to come to terms with Someone who was much bigger than his preconceived notions could ever have imagined. God's final question waits to be answered by readers of the book who dare to see themselves as Jonah and who complete Jonah's story in their own journeys through life.

■ *True to his character but not to his calling as*
■ *a prophet, Jonah refused to grant Nineveh*
■ *the right to repent. God sovereignly spared*
■ *the city, then graciously sought to teach His*
■ *equally undeserving prophet what mercy*
■ *really was. Each of us has a chance to*
■ *answer God's final question to Jonah, a ques-*
■ *tion the prophet never answered.*

QUESTIONS TO GUIDE YOUR STUDY

1. In what ways does the conversion of the sailors in chapter 1 prefigure the conversion of the Ninevites in chapter 3?

2. When Jonah objected to God's gracious protection of Nineveh, God put Jonah in Nineveh's place. How? What was this intended to teach Jonah?

3. How does God's justice fit with His compassion?

4. With whom in the story of Jonah do you identify the most? Why?

"Evil rolls across the ages, but so does good. Good has its own momentum. Corruption never wholly succeeds. (Even blasphemers acknowledge God.) Creation is stronger than sin and grace stronger still. Creation and grace are anvils that have worn out a lot of our hammers. To speak of sin by itself, to speak of it apart from the realities of creation and grace, is to forget the resolve of God.... Human sin is stubborn, but not as stubborn as the grace of God and not half so persistent, not half so ready to suffer to win its way." Cornelius Plantinga Jr., *Not the Way It's Supposed to Be: A Breviary of Sin* (Grand Rapids: Eerdmans, 1995), 199.

Perhaps the biggest miracle in the book of Jonah is not that the fish was able to save Jonah from drowning nor that a city as evil as Nineveh could repent and turn to God. Rather, the biggest miracle is that God wants to save everybody—even someone as obstinate and self-righteous as Jonah.

THE BOOK OF MICAH

STUDY OUTLINE

The book of Micah can be divided into three sections, each containing a word of judgment followed by a word of hope (1:1–2:13; 3:1–5:15; 6:1–7:20). Through Micah, God chastised the people of Israel and their leaders for fostering rampant social injustice and blatantly disregarding the standards of behavior which He had established for their lives. The solution, Micah revealed, would be in One who would come forth from Bethlehem, "whose goings forth have been from of old, from everlasting" (5:2, KJV).

JUDGMENT AND HOPE FOR GOD'S PEOPLE (1:1–2:13)

The first section of the book of Micah contains scathing words of judgment directed against the kingdoms of Israel and Judah. These are followed by brief words of hope.

A Coming Judgment (1:1–2:11)

Israel and Judah were judged for ignoring God's ways. The result was to be disaster and shame.

Judgment on the Northern Kingdom of Israel (1:1–7)

Sometimes the biblical prophets referred to the kingdoms of Israel and Judah by the names of their capital cities, Samaria and Jerusalem (e.g. Mic. 1:1, 5). Other times they called Israel, or Israel and Judah together, "Jacob," the patriarch whose twelve sons became the twelve tribes of Israel (Mic. 3:1; 5:7; cp. Gen. 29:1–30:24; 35:16–20; 49:1–27). The prophets Isaiah and Hosea also called the Northern Kingdom of Israel "Ephraim," the name of that kingdom's dominant tribe (e.g., Isa. 7:2, 9; 11:13; Hos. 5:3).

Micah prophesied against the kingdoms of Israel and Judah during the closing decades of the eighth century B.C. He used the term *Israel* in his book in several ways: to refer to the Northern Kingdom of Israel, to refer to the Southern Kingdom of Judah, and to refer to both. The kings listed in Micah 1:1, Jotham, Ahaz, and Hezekiah, reigned over Judah in Jerusalem. They, rather than the kings who ruled over Israel at the same time (Pekah and Hoshea), are listed to date the ministry of Micah because the book was written primarily with the people of Judah in mind. The Northern Kingdom of Israel fell to the Assyrians during

Micah's ministry, while Ahaz was king of Judah. The prophet Isaiah was a contemporary of Micah (cp. Isa. 1:1).

Micah opened his prophecy with a call for all the peoples of the earth to listen while God testified as a witness against Israel (v. 2). The scene was a divine court of justice held on "the high places of the earth" (v. 3), a setting to which Micah would return in chapter 6. God made a dramatic entrance into this earthly court from "His place" (1:3, NKJV), which was not only the Temple but heaven itself. Micah described God's coming in a manner that evoked the terrors of a massive earthquake: the mountains and valleys of Israel would melt "like wax before the fire" (v. 4). Physical descriptions of God's coming such as this one are called "theophanies."

The call to attention directed against the nations of the earth (1:2) and the description of natural catastrophes that attend God's coming (1:3–4) are two well-used literary motifs in the Bible. Some of the Bible's oldest poems begin with a similar call to attention (Deut. 32:1; Judg. 5:2). Isaiah, Micah's contemporary in Jerusalem, began his book in the same way (Isa. 1:2). Among the many biblical references that liken God's coming to an earthquake are Job 9:5–6, Psalm 97:1–5, and Habakkuk 3:6–7. Both motifs are found in Judges 5:3–5.

The destruction of the foundations of the earth is an appropriate way to introduce God's final judgment of the Northern Kingdom of Israel, for it pictures a reversal of the Creation of the world (cp. Job 38:4–7; Ps. 90:1–2; 104:5–9; Jer. 4:23–26; Zech. 1:2–3). God had made the earth—and especially the Promised Land, the homeland of Israel—as a special place for His own people to live and enjoy (cp. Exod. 19:5–6; Deut. 31:7–8). Now, because Israel had forsaken the ways of God, this Promised Land would be destroyed (v. 5). The mighty capital city of Samaria would become a "heap of ruins," and the rich agricultural valley lands, so painstakingly cleared of stones over the course of many generations, would return to their natural stony state (v. 6, NKJV). Most importantly, the idols of Israel would be smashed, symbolizing that Israel's efforts to reach the world of the divine through the pagan religious system of the day had come to naught (v. 7).

Within Micah's lifetime his prophecy had come true. In 722 B.C. the Assyrian king Shalmeneser V besieged and destroyed the city of Samaria, thereby ending the existence of the Northern Kingdom of Israel. Shalmeneser's son, Sargon II, claimed credit for his father's victory in the official Assyrian annals, writing, "I besieged and conquered Samaria [and] led away 27,290 inhabitants of it" (*Ancient Near Eastern Texts Relating to the Old Testament*, 2nd ed., James B. Prichard, ed. [Princeton: Princeton University Press, 1955], 284). Though Assyria was the agent, Israel was uprooted from its land by the hand of God. This reality was much more serious than Micah's portrayal of the divine earthquake that foreshadowed it (cp. 1:3–4).

Like Micah (1:7), many of the biblical prophets used the image of a harlot to illustrate Israel's unfaithfulness to God (cp. Isa. 1:21; Jer. 2:20; Ezek. 16:15–63; Hos. 1:2–3:5).

Micah's vivid description of God's coming judgment was grounded in the physical attributes of the land of Israel—mountains and valleys, vineyards and stones. He portrayed the destruction and exile of God's people as if the landscape itself had melted away.

Judgment on the Southern Kingdom of Judah (1:8–16)

Micah's response to the coming destruction of Israel was to wail and mourn (v. 8; cp. 7:1–6). The prophets regularly likened Israel to a harlot who had wantonly exposed herself. Now Micah mourned in nakedness to show *his* shame over the actions of his shameless people (v. 8; cp. Isa. 20:1–6). He wailed like a jackal and an ostrich, animals of the desert who lived far from the fertile land of Israel's promise.

The city of Beth Aphrah (NIV: Beth Ophrah; RSV: Beth-le-aphrah), literally "House of Dust," was told to roll in the dust, an extreme act of mourning (1:10; cp. Isa. 47:1; Job 42:6). The name of Lachish, the most important city in the Shephelah and Judah's second capital behind Jerusalem, sounds like the Hebrew word for the "swift steeds" that the army of Lachish would futilely send into battle (1:13). Mareshah, whose name is similar to the Hebrew word for "heir," would be possessed by an "heir" from a foreign land (1:15).

Micah also mourned because he saw that the same fate had "reached the very gate of my people, even to Jerusalem itself" (v. 9). The Southern Kingdom of Judah faced the same Assyrian threat as had Israel and deserved to be judged in the same way by the hand of God.

Micah sought to warn Judah by lamenting over the fate Jerusalem and eleven cities in the Shephelah (or "lowland"), a region of low hills lying between the mountains of Judah and the coastal Philistine plain (1:10–15; cp. Josh. 11:16). These cities were Judah's first line of defense (or "gate," 1:9) against the Assyrian juggernaut, and their inhabitants were sure to meet a violent end. The fate of many of the cities mentioned in Micah's lament was a pun in Hebrew on that city's name. Micah's own hometown of Moresheth Gath (1:14; cp. 1:1) was one of the towns that lay in the line of danger.

Micah commanded the people of Judah to shave their heads in shame over their impending destruction (v. 16). The up-and-coming generation—Judah's "precious children" (NKJV)—were about to be taken into captivity, leaving an uncertain fate for those left behind. Centuries before, Moses had warned Israel that they would be uprooted from their land if they persisted in ignoring God's ways (cp. Deut. 28:36–46; 29:25–28). Now Micah warned Judah that, just as God had used Assyria to send the Northern Kingdom of Israel into exile, so He would do to them should they, too, fail to return to Him.

The prophecies against Judah recorded in Micah 1:8–16 probably were spoken after the Northern Kingdom of Israel had fallen to Assyria in 722 B.C. Assyrian records testify that Assyrian mili-

tary campaigns were directed against the cities of
the Shephelah—including those listed in verses
10–15—during the last two decades of the
eighth century B.C. These attacks culminated in
the nearly successful attack on Jerusalem by Sennacherib in 701 B.C. The land of Judah was badly
devastated by the Assyrian army, and all of the
cities of the Shephelah were destroyed. Sennacherib claimed to have taken more than two hundred thousand people of Judah into exile.
Although the Assyrian army stood at the gate of
Jerusalem (cp. 1:12), the city did not fall because
of the faithfulness of Hezekiah, its king. With the
survival of Jerusalem, God gave the people of
Judah a second chance to be the kind of persons
He had intended them to be all along (cp. 2
Kings 18:13–19:37).

■ *Micah wailed over the fate of his people. He*
■ *wanted them to mourn over their coming*
■ *destruction, too. Perhaps if the people of*
■ *Judah were contrite, like the king of Nineveh*
■ *had been during the days of Jonah (cp. Jon.*
■ *3:6–10), God would yet spare their nation.*

Judgment on Those Who Oppress Others (2:1–11)

Micah continued his lament with what modern
interpreters of the Bible call a "woe oracle"
(2:1–2; cp. Isa. 5:8–12, 18–23; 10:1–4; 29:1–4;
15–16; Nah. 3:1–7; Hab. 2:6–19; Zeph. 3:1–5).
Such oracles, or divine answers, typically gave
the reasons the people were about to be punished by God. In this case the punishment
described in chapter 1 was coming about
because of specific acts of social injustice. Certain Israelites—those who, because of wealth or

Woe

The interjection "Woe!" sets the tone for the bad news that follows. The Hebrew word for "woe," *hoy*, is onomatopoetic; that is, it sounds like the message it is meant to convey. Sometimes *hoy* is translated "Alas!" Several times the biblical authors used the word *hoy* in contexts of mourning the dead (e.g. 1 Kings 13:30; Jer. 22:18–19; 34:5; Amos 5:16). This suggests that when the prophets used *hoy* as an interjection of woe, they were saying that because of sinful actions, the people of Israel were as good as dead (cp. Rom. 6:23).

power, were able to do so—were taking the landed property of others by premeditated force (2:1–2).

Each Israelite family had been given its own inheritance in the land of Israel. This land gave a family its security from generation to generation. To lose one's inheritance was to lose one's place in the world (cp. Lev. 25:33–34; Num. 36:7–9). To lose one's inheritance because a fellow Israelite *stole* it, as King Ahab did with Naboth—was anathema, for it was tantamount to sending that person into exile (cp. 1 Kings 21:1–16; Isa. 5:8–10).

God's reply was that while the Israelites had been "devising iniquity" against others (2:1, NKJV), He had been "devising disaster" against them (2:3, NKJV). A reversal of fortunes such as this—evil heaped upon the evildoers—was a common theme in the prophets (cp. Nah. 3:8–15; Hab. 2:6–8, 15–17). The reality behind the imagery of verse 3 can be found on Assyrian reliefs depicting battle scenes showing captive prisoners of war, doomed to a lifetime of slavery in a foreign land, being led away with chains around their necks. Israel had been given their land by God (cp. Gen. 13:14–18; Josh. 1:1–9; 13:1–21:45); now He was going to take away their heritage (2:4), leaving no one to see that the boundaries of each person's estate were protected (2:5).

Micah's audience responded in verse 6: "Don't preach at us," they chided. "Such disaster can't possibly come" because, they implied, "we are God's special people" (the NIV is more clear than the NKJV in this verse). Micah replied that God promises to do good "to him whose ways are upright" (2:7). Later he would again remind

Israel that all God wants His people to do is "act justly, and to love mercy and to walk humbly" with Him (6:8).

Rather than follow Him, God's people had "risen up as an enemy;" that is, they had become their own worst enemy (2:8, NKJV). By seizing land that was not theirs, they had in effect sent their fellow Israelites—women and children—off into exile, out of the special environment that God had prepared for them (2:9). The God-ordained chain of spiritual education, from parent to child to grandchild (cp. Deut. 6:6–9) was broken, with the tragic result that "you have taken away My glory forever" (2:9, NKJV). Micah told Israel that they might just as well leave their land voluntarily, for it was no longer the safe and secure place of rest that God had intended it to be (2:10).

As a parting shot at his insolent audience, Micah declared that the prophet who best suited their self-absorbed interests was a liar who would "prophesy to you of wine and drink" (2:11, NKJV). The Israelites were, after all, already acting as if they were drunk (cp. Job 12:24–25; Joel 1:5; Hab. 2:15–17).

By leading Israel out of Egypt and into the Promised Land, Moses and Joshua gave "rest" to God's people (Deut. 12:9–10; Josh. 1:12–15; 11:23; cp. Mic. 2:10). This rest was to be reminiscent of the "rest" which God experienced after creating the world (Gen. 2:1–3) and which characterized life in the Garden of Eden. Jesus spoke of the inward aspects of this rest when He called "all you who labor and are heavy laden" to take upon themselves his yoke (not the burdensome yoke of oxen or even the neck chains of a conquering army) and thereby find rest for their souls (Matt. 11:28–30). The writer of Hebrews spoke of the final, heavenly rest which awaits all who find their rest in Jesus (Heb. 4:1–13).

- ■ Micah wailed aloud over the personal and
- ■ social sins of his people. The society that they
- ■ had built groaned with injustice. God was
- ■ sending judgment, but His people were too
- ■ blind—whether apathetic or self-righteous,
- ■ it didn't matter—even to know that anything
- ■ was wrong.

A Future Hope (2:12–13)

Yet there was hope. God was allowing judgment to come but would "surely gather . . . the remnant of Israel" and put them, like sheep, into the fold of His protective care (2:12, RSV). One from among the sheep would make a breech in the wall of the sheepfold and lead the rest of the sheep out in a victorious march (2:13). This one is called "their king," and is closely identified with the Lord who is "at their head."

Three themes found in verses 12 and 13 are prominent in the Old Testament.

- A faithful remnant of persons who are able to maintain a genuine relationship with God stands as the true heir to all of the divine promises (cp. Gen. 7:23; Num. 26:65; 1 Kings 19:14–18; Isa. 6:13; 46:3–4; Amos 3:12).

- God is the Divine Shepherd, and the people of Israel are His sheep (Ps. 23:1–6; 78:52–54; Isa. 40:11; Ezek. 34:11–24; Zech. 10:3; 11:7–17). The New Testament writers developed this imagery when they portrayed Jesus as the Good Shepherd (Matt. 9:36; John 10:11–18; Heb. 13:20).

- A victorious Messiah will lead the remnant of God's people back to Himself (cp. Isa. 49:5–6). Although Micah does not use the word *Messiah*, it is clear that the one leading the sheep in 2:13 is the Messiah spoken of often by other prophets. This Messiah would come from among the people of Israel yet be able to do things that all previous Israelites were incapable of doing. He would also have a special relationship with the Lord (2:13). Micah speaks more about this coming One in chapter 5.

In any given generation most of those who consider themselves to be God's people fail to follow Him, while a few, His spiritual heirs, remain faithful. God always sees to it that this remnant, composed of the ones through whom He can work, survives even periods of divine judgment.

- Judgment may indeed come, but hope was
- certain. God was preserving a faithful rem-
- nant that His Messiah would lead in victori-
- ous procession. Micah's words of hope
- anticipate the work of Jesus.

QUESTIONS TO GUIDE YOUR STUDY

1. How did Micah use the world of nature to explain God's dealings with people? Why is this an effective way to communicate?
2. How did Micah's view of justice differ from that of his audience?
3. Micah spoke in bold terms—life, death, judgment, and war. How can these concepts be used to communicate to modern audiences that are complacent about such issues?

JUDGMENT AND HOPE FOR GOD'S LEADERS (3:1–5:15)

The second part of the book of Micah contains words of judgment directed against the leaders of ancient Israel and Judah. These are followed by a lengthy section which describes the glorious future hope of Zion.

A Coming Judgment (3:1–12)

Micah judged the leaders of Israel and Judah for treating their people violently under the pretext of justice and righteousness.

Judgment on God's Leaders in Israel (vv. 1–4)

Having delivered God's words of judgment on the people of Israel and Judah, Micah now turned to their leaders. The "heads of Jacob and rulers of the house of Israel" (3:1, RSV) refers to the leaders of both the Northern Kingdom of

Written records from across the ancient Near East speak of the ideal king as one who provided justice for those who were poor, needy, and helpless. For the psalmist this ideal king was God: "Blessed is he whose help is the God of Jacob. . . . He upholds the cause of the oppressed and gives food to the hungry. . . . sustains the fatherless and the widow, but he frustrates the ways of the wicked" (Ps. 146:5–9).

"Let not many of you become teachers, my brethren, for you know that we who teach shall be judged with greater strictness. For we all make many mistakes" (James 3:1–2, RSV).

Israel and the Southern Kingdom of Judah (cp. 3:9–10, where the same titles are used in connection with Jerusalem).

God holds leaders to a higher standard of accountability than He does those whom they lead. Leaders are expected to know what justice is and strive to uphold it throughout all levels of society. This social dynamic was missing in Micah's day. Israel's leaders had not only failed to uphold justice, but they also were the very ones who were acting unjustly (vv. 1–2). In one of the most horrifying passages of the entire Bible, Micah described them as behaving like cannibals (3:2–3; cp. Ps. 14:4; 27:2; Ezek. 11:3; 34:1–3).

The people of Israel, silent and helpless in the face of a calculatingly unjust judiciary, could cry only to the Lord (cp. Ps. 34:15–18; 59:1–2; 82:1–4). Micah saw that Israel's leaders, too, would cry to God when divine judgment turned against them but that God would respond just as they had to their people and "hide His face from them" (v. 4, NKJV). He has no tolerance for hypocrisy.

■ *The leaders of ancient Israel ignored the*
■ *basic social needs of their people. In doing so,*
■ *they devoured the persons for whom they*
■ *were supposed to provide. Ignoring their*
■ *responsibilities, they were in turn ignored by*
■ *God.*

Judgment on God's Prophets in Israel
  (vv. 5–8)

Micah reserved special words of judgment for Israel's prophets. Because he was God's true prophet, Micah was especially sensitive to the way false prophets had led the people of Israel astray. If their listeners took good care of the prophets' physical needs, the prophets said what the people wanted to hear and cried, "peace!" But if the Israelites did not treat the prophets well materially, the prophets "declared war" against them (v. 5, RSV). Prophets were supposed to speak the words of God irrespective of popular opinion. Instead, they not only allowed themselves to be "bought," but they also insisted on it (cp. 2 Tim. 4:3).

Micah declared that the sun would go down on prophets of his day (v. 6), and that without access to divine light they would face public shame and disgrace (v. 7). A common biblical image pictured Israelites who were unresponsive to God's Word as sitting and walking in darkness (cp. Isa. 6:9–10; 8:21–9:2). Because the prophets of Micah's day lacked vision, they were as sightless as the people they were supposed to guide.

Micah used the false prophets of his day as a foil to present his own credentials to Israel. He was filled with precisely what the others lacked: power, justice, might, and, above all, the Spirit of the Lord (v. 8). Given these divine resources, his job was to point out the sin of others. Micah spoke in an age when everyone was trying to convince everyone else that things were really OK just the way they were. The response to Micah's words was as predictable as it would be if he brought the same message today.

Peace

The Hebrew word for peace, *shalom,* means much more than just a cessation of hostilities. At its core, *shalom* means "wholeness." It includes concepts such as wellness, health, prosperity, completeness, harmony, and safety. Individuals, societies, and nations should all strive for *shalom* in every relationship. Sin is the absence of *shalom.*

"The prophet is a man who feels fiercely. God has thrust a burden on his soul, and he is bowed and stunned at man's fierce greed. Frightful is the agony of man; no human voice can convey its full terror. Prophecy is the voice that God has lent to the silent agony, a voice to the plundered poor, to the profaned riches of the world. It is a form of living, a crossing point of God and man. God is raging in the prophet's words."
Abraham Heschel, *The Prophets,* vol. 1 (New York: Harper Torchbooks, 1962), 5.

■ *The prophets of Micah's day used their posi-*
■ *tions to further their own status in society.*
■ *The result was public shame. In sharp con-*
■ *trast, Micah stood true, filled with the Spirit*
■ *of the Lord and boldly pointing out the real-*
■ *ity of sin.*

Jerusalem was not destroyed in Micah's day (cp. 2 Kings 19:1–37), but one hundred years later the Babylonians again threatened the city. This time God told the prophet Jeremiah that Jerusalem would fall. The people, priests, and prophets of Jerusalem arrested Jeremiah for preaching a message that they did not want to hear. In order to justify their belief in the inviolability of their city, they quoted Micah 3:12 (Jer. 26:16–19). The argument was simple: if Micah had said that Jerusalem would fall and it didn't, why then should they believe Jeremiah when he said the same thing? God had spared Jerusalem in Micah's day when King Hezekiah threw himself on the mercy of God. However, in Jeremiah's day neither the king nor the people Judah were willing to do the same.

An Additional Judgment on God's Leaders in Israel (vv. 9–12)

Micah again addressed the leaders of Israel, mentioning in particular the heads (civil officials), the priests, and the prophets (v. 11). Together these represented the three primary institutions of authority in ancient Israel. All were supposed to serve the people selflessly and responsibly; all had prostituted their offices by regularly selling out to the highest bidder (vv. 9–10).

These leaders of Israel were particularly culpable because they were using the Lord as a front to justify their activities (v. 11). Bible interpreters suggest that during Micah's day ancient Israel held to a "royal Zion theology" in which God had promised that neither this Temple nor His chosen holy city of Jerusalem would ever be destroyed, irrespective of the behavior of the Israelites. God *had* promised to be with Israel, it is true (Gen. 28:15; Num. 6:24; Deut. 31:6, 8; Ps. 121:7–8), but Micah's contemporaries had forgotten—conveniently, for their cause—that divine blessings were conditional upon human response (cp. Deut. 28:1–68).

Micah preached the unthinkable: God was indeed willing for the city of Jerusalem to fall to a foreign army in order to judge Israel's institutionalized unrighteousness (v. 12). The images of a "plowed field" and a "wooded height" are prophetic overstatements intended to convey the seriousness of the situation that Israel faced. By destroying their nation, God sought to teach His people that efforts to create a just society based solely on human efforts can't work. Jerusalem would be destroyed, but out of its ashes the hope for a society of peace based on God's righteousness would arise. To this hope Micah now turned in detail.

- The leaders of Micah's day were trying to use
- God as a tool to bolster their own power and
- wealth. Society had become so
- twisted—from the top on down—that the
- only solution was to destroy Jerusalem so
- that God could begin again in forming an
- Israel that followed Him.

A Future Hope (4:1–5:15)

In the next two chapters, Micah spelled out the reasons for, and character of, Israel's hope. A Ruler from Bethlehem was coming who would purify Israel and lead them to true righteousness and peace.

The Exaltation of Zion (4:1–8)

Micah saw a bright and glorious future for Israel, a future that "shall come to pass in the latter days" (v. 1, RSV). The phrase "the latter days" was used by biblical writers to refer to what many Bible readers call the "Messianic Age," a time in the far future when God would raise up His Messiah and bring about the spiritual and national redemption of Israel (e.g., Num. 24:14; Deut. 31:29; Jer. 30:24; Ezek. 38:16; Dan.

Micah 4:1–3 is also found in Isaiah 2:2–4. It is impossible to know which of these prophets borrowed the passage from the other, or if both took it from a third source. Because Micah and Isaiah were contemporaries, it is clear that this passage must have been well-known in their day. Isaiah used the passage to introduce his entire book, while Micah used it to introduce his book's climax.

10:14). The "latter days" began with the birth of Jesus and will end at His Second Coming in power and glory.

Micah characterized Israel's glorious future in several ways:

- Jerusalem, here called Zion (v. 2), would become the spiritual capital of the world. Micah pictured the elevation of the "mountain" of "the house of the Lord"—the Temple mount, which is topographically lower than the hills immediately to the east, north, and west—to signify the increased spiritual influence of Jerusalem. People from across the world would eagerly stream to Jerusalem to learn what God requires of them. The words "His ways," "His paths," "the law," and "the word of the Lord" (v. 2, NKJV) are all well-known biblical terms used to describe the positive aspects of God's revelation to humankind. Thus the priestly function of the Temple would give way to the prophetic.

- The coming Messianic Age would be an age without poverty or fear. Resources which had been used for war would now be used for peace (v. 3). God's people would enjoy domestic tranquillity, as seen in the classic pastoral image of every man sitting quietly "under his vine and under his fig tree" (v. 4, RSV; cp. 1 Kings 4:25).

- God would restore the remnant of His people to Himself (vv. 5–7; cp. 2:12–13; 5:7–9). Micah pictured this remnant as persons who had been lame and afflicted, an appropriate characterization for those who in his day were unable to "walk in [God's] paths" (cp. 4:2). God would "assemble" the remnant and make them into a "strong nation" (v. 7), clear testimony to His power and the sheer inability of people to help themselves (cp. Ezek. 34:16; Zeph. 3:19).

■ *Micah saw a day when God would restore*
■ *His people to favor so that they could live in*
■ *peace. The nations of the world would be*
■ *drawn to God through Jerusalem, where they*
■ *would learn how to walk in His ways.*

The Oppression and Deliverance of Zion (4:9–5:6)

But this glorious future was far from reality in Micah's day. In order to underscore the stark contrast between the harsh conditions of the present and the glorious future of the latter days, Micah's prophecy alternated between scenes of gloom (4:9–11; 5:1, 3) and glory (4:12–13; 5:2, 4–6).

Micah began this section by speaking of the coming Babylonian Exile (4:9–10). In his day Assyria, not Babylon, posed a threat of world conquest. Nevertheless Micah, like Isaiah, foresaw that Jerusalem would instead fall to Babylon (4:10; cp. Isa. 48:14, 20; 2 Kings 24:1–25:26). Facing destruction, the people of Zion would "writhe and groan" like a woman in labor (4:10, RSV; cp. Matt. 24:7–8). Someday a woman in labor would give birth to a Ruler who would restore Israel to God's favor (cp. 5:2–3). In the meantime Israel would leave Jerusalem for the "open field" (4:10), far from the security of city and home, in effect undoing the Exodus from Egypt and the conquest of Canaan.

The origin of the word *Zion* is unknown but may be related to a word for fortress. Jerusalem was called the "stronghold of Zion" in the account of David's conquest of the city (2 Sam. 5:7, RSV). In Solomon's day the term *Zion* was extended to include the Temple mount (cp. Ps. 9:11). Eventually, as Jerusalem spread to encompass the hill to the west, *Zion* came to designate the entire city (Ps. 69:35). The name *Zion* was taken over by early Christians who saw themselves as the new people of God in order to designate the area within Jerusalem where the early church was born (Acts 2:1–42). This area, now outside of the walls of the old city of Jerusalem, is still known as Mount Zion today.

Perhaps one of the reasons Jesus healed so many persons who were lame was to signal that He was the one sent by God to show people how to "walk in God's paths" (cp. Matt. 11:5; 15:30; John 5:2–14).

Micah spoke of the nations gathered against Israel for war (4:11). The nations thought they had Jerusalem trapped, but, according to divine plan, God revealed that He had allowed them to gather around Jerusalem in order to trap *them* (4:12). The nations were nothing more than sheaves of grain gathered onto a threshing floor, which Israel, the "daughter of Zion," was going to thresh thoroughly (4:13, RSV). Isaiah used the same image to describe the future work of Israel (Isa. 41:14–16). According to Micah, Israel would devote the threshed grain—the wealth of the nations—to the Lord, paying homage to Him rather than using it to enrich themselves (4:13). This picture was a far cry from the present reality in which Jerusalem stood to be destroyed because of the greed of its leaders (cp. 3:9–12).

The first line of 5:1 is difficult in Hebrew, and various English translations differ significantly. Yet the overall sense is clear: Israel was under attack, the city of Jerusalem besieged, and its leader, or "judge," was humiliated. This is evidently a reference to the Assyrian siege of Jerusalem in 701 B.C., when Sennacherib's emissary publicly taunted the Judean king Hezekiah (cp. 2 Kings 18:13–37).

Hope would come, but from an unexpected place. Out of Bethlehem Ephrathah, home to one of the smallest clans of Judah, would come a Ruler whose rights to the throne reached back "from ancient days"(5:2, RSV). This reference to antiquity pointed at least to the days of David (cp. Amos 9:11) if not the origin of humankind (cp. Rom. 5:14). Micah saw the re-establishment of a strong and effective Davidic kingdom—an important element in the developing stream of Messianic prophecy—but recognized that Israel must first suffer at the hands of a foreign enemy (5:3).

Micah compared the work of the coming Ruler from Bethlehem—the Messiah, although this term is not used here—to that of a strong and caring shepherd (5:4). The image of a shepherd is appropriate given the shepherding background of David (cp. 1 Sam. 16:11; 17:28, 34–36), and anticipates the ministry of Jesus (Matt. 9:36; John 10:11, 14; Heb. 13:20).

But Micah also spoke to the immediate needs of his contemporaries. Israel would be delivered from the Assyrians by "seven shepherds and eight princes of men" (5:5, RSV). The sequence of numbers "seven . . . eight" was a Hebrew idiom that referred to an unspecified yet adequately large number of leaders who would act in a way that would foreshadow the even greater work of the coming Messianic shepherd. With God's help, they would stem the Assyrian advance into Judah.

According to Genesis 35:16–20, Rachel died in childbirth at Ephrath (an alternative spelling of Ephrathah), which probably was either another name for Bethlehem or the name of a district lying within or adjacent to Bethlehem (cp. Gen. 35:19). Ephrathah may originally have been the name of a clan of Judah (cp. 1 Chron. 2:24) that settled in the vicinity of Bethlehem.

Matthew referred to Micah 5:2 and several other Old Testament passages in his narrative of Jesus' birth in order to show that Jesus fulfilled Messianic prophecies (Matt. 1:22–23—cp. Isa. 7:14; Matt. 2:5–6—cp. Mic. 5:2 and 2 Sam. 5:2; Matt. 2:17–18—cp. Jer. 31:15).

- *In the midst of unsettled times Micah saw a*
- *day when God would send a Ruler who*
- *would deliver His people from harm. Mat-*
- *thew recognized this One to be Jesus (Matt.*
- *2:5–6). In the meantime, Micah offered hope*
- *that Israel would be able to withstand the*
- *Assyrians threat.*

The Purified Remnant of Zion (5:7–15)

At the end of this lengthy section of hope, Micah returned to an important theme in his prophetic message, the remnant that God would restore in Israel (vv. 7–9). Previously he had compared the restored remnant to sheep in a fold (2:12)

In Israel it does not rain from early May until October. Yet during this time standing grain ripens, and juicy, plump grapes form on the vine. This happens because during the clear, cool nights of summer the moisture-rich air of the Mediterranean Sea condenses on trees and plants in the hills and valleys throughout the Israeli countryside. Dew was seen as God's blessing on Israel (Hos. 14:5; cp. 1 Kings 17:1). Moses likened it to uplifting speech (Deut. 32:2).

Asherah was the pagan goddess of fertility worshiped throughout the ancient Near East. The Asherim of Micah 5:14 were sacred poles and other images erected as objects of worship. They were placed on high hills or under the shade of green trees where devotees of Asherah could congregate and pay homage to her purported ability to bring fertility to the land (2 Kings 17:10; Jer. 17:2).

and to lame people who would be made into a strong nation (4:6–7). Now Micah likened the remnant of Israel to two forces in nature, one gentle and the other quite fierce. In one sense the remnant of Israel would be like dew or a shower upon grass, a quiet blessing that brings life to the nations (v. 7). The remnant of Israel would also be like a lion that tears and devours its prey (vv. 8–9). In the same way, Israel would eventually overcome its enemies to live in peace.

The remnant would survive, but in a radically altered environment. Things Israel believed were necessary for survival in Micah's day would have no place in God's restored nation. These included "horses," "chariots," "cities," and "strongholds," armaments and technology used for war (vv. 10–11. NKJV). King Hezekiah had vastly increased Judah's military capacity in hopes of being able to withstand the Assyrian siege. Micah and Isaiah responded that human efforts at self-survival are futile if no thought is given to God (cp. Isa. 22:8–11).

Also excluded from God's kingdom were "sorceries," "soothsayers," "images" and "pillars," man-made images that Israel thought brought them closer to the world of the divine (vv. 12–15, NKJV). All of these were part and parcel of the religious system of the Canaanites and Israel's neighbors. Kings and generals of the ancient Near East normally consulted their gods through various means of divination, thereby hoping to control or at least predict the outcome of events. These had no place in God's kingdom, where people, nature, and events were under the control and care of their Creator.

N

■ *God was not through with His people in spite*
■ *of the well-deserved punishment they faced.*
■ *He promised to purify and restore Israel to*
■ *favor and help them to see that real peace*
■ *comes not from human self-effort but from*
■ *trust in God.*

QUESTIONS TO GUIDE YOUR STUDY

1. What is peace? According to Micah, what are the things that make for peace?
2. How can Christians understand and appreciate Micah's prophecy that Jerusalem would become the spiritual capital of the world?
3. How did Micah's prophecies add to the Israelites' growing understanding of the Messiah?

JUDGMENT AND HOPE FOR GOD'S PEOPLE (6:1–7:20)

The final part of the book of Micah, like the first two, contains scathing judgment followed by an announcement of hope. As is typical for the biblical prophets, hope always gets in the last word.

A Coming Judgment (6:1–7:6)

God brought a lawsuit against Israel because they had been unfaithful to His covenant. Found guilty, He pronounced sentence upon them. Micah responded by wailing in distress over the bleak future of his people.

God's Lawsuit Against Israel (6:1–16)

The covenant lawsuit is a form of biblical prophecy in which God brings formal charges against His people for repeatedly violating the terms of His covenant. Similar lawsuits are found in Isaiah 1:2–9; 3:13–15; Jeremiah

2:9–13, and Hosea 4:1–3. They follow a pattern common to ancient Near Eastern court settings in which witnesses are called, evidence against the accused given, a defense offered, and a verdict reached. As is His right, God typically sat as both judge and prosecuting attorney.

Reminiscent of the way in which the book of Micah began, God first called the mountains to stand as a silent jury against Israel (6:1–2; cp. 1:2–3). In an emotional plea, He opened His prosecution by asking what He had done to deserve such ill treatment by His people (v. 3). The backhanded question, "How have I wearied you?" (NKJV) was clearly meant to prod the people into realizing that *they* were the ones who had wearied *Him* (cp. Isa. 43:24).

In Amos 3:9, God called the nations of Assyria and Egypt to assemble themselves on the mountains that surrounded Samaria, the capital of the Northern Kingdom of Israel, to witness "the great tumults . . . and oppressions in her midst" (RSV). These mountains are higher in elevation than is the hill on which Samaria sat, providing a natural amphitheater for the high drama taking place behind the walls of Israel's capital. God called the mountains themselves to witness against Israel in Micah 6.

God then quickly reviewed the history of the Exodus from Egypt (vv. 4–5). He had graciously given Moses, Aaron, and Miriam to be Israel's leaders, thwarted Balak's attempt to curse Israel through the prophet Balaam (cp. Num. 22–24), and brought Israel safely from Shittim east of the Jordan River to Gilgal in Canaan, their Promised Land (Josh. 3–4). God did not mention that all the while the Israelites had grumbled and complained.

The Israelites had assumed that, by offering God the right combination of sacrifices, they could please Him in spite of their moral shortcomings. Believing this, they evidently interrupted God's prosecution speech and, in self-defense, reminded Him of their perfunctory religious devotion. Their self-deception prompted Micah to continue the lawsuit on God's behalf. He reminded Israel that without a proper heart commitment, even excessive acts of sacrifice are worthless (v. 7). The Israelites already knew what they should be doing (v. 8; cp. Ps. 51:15–19), which made their obstinacy all the more serious. Micah's admonition to "do justice, . . . love kindness and . . . walk humbly with your God" (RSV) summed up the social and moral obligations which underlay not only his prophecy but also the entire Old Testament (cp. Lev. 19:17–18; Deut. 6:5; Ps. 15:1–5; 24:3–6).

God then passed judgment. He was both unable and unwilling to overlook the "treasures of wickedness in the house of the wicked" (v. 10, RSV). Israel was socially and morally corrupt, shot through with institutionalized injustice (vv. 11–12; cp. Amos 8:4–6). The basis of God's sentence was unchanged from chapters 2 and 3, in which Micah had blasted Israel and its leaders for sins of the marketplace—shady business dealings which in God's eyes were crimes against humanity.

Israel's punishment would hit them where they would feel it the most. God's blessings of abundance and prosperity, promised to those who kept His covenant stipulations (Deut. 28:1–14), would be taken away. Rather than keep the statutes of God, Israel had "kept the statutes of Omri, and all the works of the house of Ahab" his son (v. 16, RSV), the Israelite kings who, through an unholy economic alliance with the Phoenicians, had established Baalism as the state-sponsored religion of Israel (cp. 1 Kings 16:29–22:40). As a result, the people of Israel would work hard, try to save money, and eat well, but have only hunger and want to show for it (vv. 14–15). They would become a mockery among the nations (v. 16; cp. 2:4), totally unable to fulfill their original commission to bring God's blessing to all the peoples of the earth (cp. Gen. 12:3). God's people had

"Self-deception is a shadowy phenomenon by which we pull the wool over some part of our own psyche. We put a move on ourselves. We deny, suppress, or minimize what we know to be true. We assert, adorn, and elevate what we know to be false. We prettify ugly realities and sell ourselves the prettified versions. . . . We become our own dupes, playing the role of both perpetrator and victim. . . . We actually forget that certain things are wrong and that we have done them. To the extent that we are self-deceived, we occupy a twilight zone in which we make up reality as we go along, a twilight zone in which the shortest distance between two points is a labyrinth." Cornelius Plantinga Jr., *Not the Way Its Supposed to Be: A Breviary of Sin* (Grand Rapids: Eerdmans, 1995), 105.

failed in their mission to be a special covenant people. Micah could do nothing but wail in agony and shame.

■ *Because covenant unfaithfulness had become*
■ *an accepted way of life in Israel, God took*
■ *His own people to court. There they were*
■ *tried and found wanting. God passed judg-*
■ *ment on Israel, sentencing them to an exist-*
■ *ence of misery and shame.*

Micah's Lament over Israel's Doom (7:1–6)
The first six verses of Micah 7 are a formal lament. The speaker is not identified but can be best understood as Micah, wailing on behalf of the people of Israel.

In his lament, Micah selected several incidents or objects from everyday life to illustrate Israel's sad condition:

- The fields and vineyards of Israel had been stripped bare, leaving nothing for the hungry or poor to glean (v. 1; cp. Deut. 24:19–22; Ruth 2:1–23). By implication, Israel had been stripped of righteousness, and no good person remained in the land (v. 2; cp. Jer. 5:1–5; Ezek. 22:30).
- People had become both predator and prey, ambushing one another as a hunter would capture a wild animal (v. 2).
- The leaders of Israel schemed together (literally "wove their plans together as if making a cord," v. 3) to use the justice system for personal gain. The most righteous were no better than a hedge of sharp thorns, good only to rip and tear their people apart (v. 4).

- Neighbors, friends, and even close family members could no longer be trusted (vv. 5–6).

The very foundations of society had collapsed, eliminating any chance that Israel might have had to withstand a foreign invasion.

■ *God wanted His people to be a loving and*
■ *caring community and had given them His*
■ *covenant to help teach them how to live.*
■ *Instead, Israelite society had rotted; and*
■ *Micah, knowing what should have been the*
■ *best, wept over the worst.*

A Future Hope (7:7–20)

As is the case with most of the minor prophets, Micah ended his book with a word of hope. He spoke of Israel's need to bear their punishment and wait patiently for God. Eventually God would restore His people to favor and give them the blessings that He had intended them to have all along.

A Believer's Confidence (vv. 7–10)

Micah knew what was coming and chose to stand firm. He decided to wait for "the God of my salvation" to bring deliverance (v. 7, RSV), enduring the trouble rather than fighting back or looking for a way to escape. In doing so, he stood at crosscurrents with society. As at the beginning of chapter 7, Micah spoke on behalf of Israel; he said and felt what he wanted his people to say and feel, all the while knowing that his preaching was having little effect.

Micah knew that his people would fall to their enemies. Yet verses 8–10, a psalm of trust, were spoken in the assurance that even though

Jesus alluded to the topsy-turvy family relationships of Micah 7:6 to describe the advent of the Messianic age (Matt. 10:21, 35–36). His message would be so controversial among the established Jewish and Gentile communities that people would be rejected by their own family and friends if they believed in Him.

The phrase "but as for me" which opens verse 7 indicates Micah's resolve, a conviction that was as strong as was Joshua's when Israel's greatest general faced his people with the challenge "choose you this day whom ye will serve . . . but as for me and my house, we will serve the Lord" (Josh. 24:15, KJV).

"Perseverance is more than endurance. It is endurance combined with absolute assurance and certainty that what we are looking for is going to happen. Perseverance means more than just hanging on, which may be only exposing our fear of letting go and falling. Perseverance is our supreme effort of refusing to believe that our Hero is going to be conquered." Oswald Chambers, *My Utmost for His Highest*, Oswald Chambers Publications Association, Ltd., 22 Feb. 1992.

The River

The "River" (v. 12, RSV) from which people will come to Israel is the Euphrates River in northwestern Mesopotamia (modern western Iraq and northern Syria). The Euphrates was such a dominant landmark in the ancient Near East that in biblical Hebrew it was simply called "the River."

Israel's enemies would stand in triumph ultimately they would not prevail. Israel's root problem was human sin (v. 9), which had so polluted and weakened the fabric of society that its collapse was inevitable. Israel would indeed fall, Micah knew, but before long its enemies, too, would topple and "be trodden down like the mire of the streets" (v. 10, RSV).

§N

- Israel had to walk through what David had
- called "the valley of the shadow of death"
- (Ps. 23:4). Micah looked forward to the day
- when God would bring His people back into
- the light of His salvation (7:9).

The Assurance of Victory (vv. 11–20)

Micah saw a day when Israel would rise to world prominence among the nations. In chapter 4 he had spoken of the glorious elevation of Jerusalem as the spiritual capital of the world (4:1–4; cp. Isa. 2:2–4). Now he added important details about the restoration of Israel. The walls of Israel's cities would be rebuilt, signaling freedom and the end of foreign oppression (v. 11). The boundary of Israel would be enlarged, indicating prosperity and strength as in the days of Solomon (v. 11; cp. 1 Kings 4:21). Finally, so many people from across the world would come to Israel that, by comparison, the earth would seem desolate (vv. 12–13). It is not clear if these people were those who had been in Exile and were returning to their homeland, or Gentiles who, as in Micah 4:1–2, were attracted to God through the witness of His people in Israel. In either case, God's age-old promise that all the nations of the earth will be blessed through Israel will be fulfilled (cp. Gen. 12:3).

Verse 14 is a prayer that God might again care for His people as He did in former times, when they first entered the Promised Land. Bashan (the modern Golan Heights) and Gilead (today the highlands of Jordan north of Amman) are fertile regions where sheep can enjoy a life of ease. Both were part of the land apportioned to the tribes of Israel by Moses and Joshua (cp. Deut. 3:1–17; Josh. 13:1–33). For Micah, Bashan and Gilead represented God's generosity and blessing.

God replied that He would indeed show His people marvelous things just as He had done "when you came out of the land of Egypt" (v. 15, RSV), early in His covenant relationship with them. The motif of starting over again is common in the prophets and reflects God's goodness, mercy, and commitment to His people (cp. Hos. 2:14–20). Upon seeing the mighty hand of God restore the fortunes of Israel, the nations will be silenced and fall in humiliation and dread before the Lord (vv. 16–17).

The last three verses of the book of Micah are a doxology (or hymn) of praise answering the question, "Who is a God like you?" (v. 18). Micah's audience was confused and troubled over the future that God had in store for them. They no doubt asked why God would allow the kind of trouble Micah claimed He was sending when they were, after all, His chosen people. In a series of marvelous phrases describing the merciful character of God, Micah responded that God delights in showing favor to His people (vv. 18–20). And among His greatest acts of compassion, God promised to "hurl all our sins into the depths of the sea" (7:19).

Micah said that the nations would bow before God upon witnessing the restoration of Israel (7:16–17). The apostle Paul noted that the same thing would happen at the exultation of Jesus: "Therefore God has highly exalted him and bestowed on him the name which is above every name, that at the name of Jesus every knee should bow, in heaven and on earth and under the earth, and every tongue confess that Jesus Christ is Lord, to the glory of God the Father" (Phil. 2:9–11, RSV).

■ *Judgment may come, but God promises to see*
■ *His people through. Micah spoke of a day*
■ *when God would forgive Israel's sins and*
■ *restore them to favor. This He has done*
■ *through Jesus, the Ruler who Micah foresaw*
■ *would bring peace to Israel (cp. 5:2–4).*

QUESTIONS TO GUIDE YOUR STUDY

1. Why was using a covenant lawsuit a particularly effective way for Micah to address his audience?
2. How can the disintegration of a society be considered the judgment of God?
3. What does God require of those who are committed to Him? How do we short-change God?

THE BOOK OF NAHUM

STUDY OUTLINE

The book of Nahum teaches that God punishes sin. God directed His righteous anger toward Nineveh, the capital city of Assyria, ancient Israel's greatest enemy. The Assyrians had already destroyed the Northern Kingdom of Israel, and for decades they had threatened to obliterate Judah as well. In order to encourage the people of Judah, Nahum prophesied the coming destruction of Nineveh. At the same time, he also sought to warn his people that they could face the same future should they continue to act no better than the nations around them.

THE DOOM OF NINEVEH (1:1–15)

Nahum sang praises to the power of God, then proceeded to call down divine vengeance on Nineveh. At the same time, he looked forward to a day when the people of Judah would live in peace.

A Hymn to the Power of God (vv. 1–8)

The little that can be gleaned from the Bible about the life of Nahum is found in 1:1. Nahum's name means "comfort," which is

Nineveh, located above the upper Tigris River, was some five hundred miles northeast of Israel. The vast ruins of the ancient site lie near the city of Mosul in northern Iraq. Nineveh became the official capital of Assyria during the reign of Sennacherib, the Assyrian king who nearly destroyed Jerusalem in 701 B.C. (cp. 2 Kings 18:13–19:37). Sennacherib rebuilt the city to rival the greatest cities of antiquity, creating a veritable "wonder of the ancient world." The discovery of the vast library of Ashurbanipal, Sennacherib's grandson and the last great king of Assyria, in the ruins of Nineveh brought to light the rich Assyrian literary tradition. Nahum probably prophesied during the reign of Ashurbanipal.

appropriate given the turmoil and fear which Israel experienced whenever the Assyrian army was on the prowl (cp. Isa. 40:1). Some Bible interpreters have tried to identify Elkosh (1:1), Nahum's home, with Capernaum (lit. "the village of Nahum"), but this is unlikely. Nahum evidently prophesied during Assyria's last burst of terror-filled energy; within a few short decades Nineveh fell to a combined army of Babylonians and Medes, marking its end as an Assyrian city.

Nahum's opening hymn sets the stage for the entire book. God is portrayed as "jealous," "avenging" and "wrathful" (v. 2, RSV), characteristics that proclaim He will tolerate no rivals. Although "slow to anger," God will, when necessary, exercise His great might and "by no means clear the guilty" (v. 3, RSV; cp. Jonah 4:2). One hundred years before Nahum prophesied against Nineveh, Assyria had destroyed the Northern Kingdom of Israel and herded its people into exile (2 Kings 17:1–6). Although broken and decimated, Israel was still God's covenant people. By promising to destroy Assyria, God was vindicating His covenant and acting on Israel's behalf.

Nahum used the language of natural disasters to describe the vindication of God (vv. 3–5). He likened God's coming to an earthquake and a scorching wind off the desert, sapping life out of the land (cp. Hab. 3:3–7). Even Bashan (the modern Golan Heights), Mount Carmel, and Lebanon, regions of great rainfall and natural bounty, whither under the breath of God (cp. Amos 1:2).

If the mountains melt before God, what hope is there for people (1:5–6; cp. Mic. 1:4–5)?

Nahum reminded his audience that God is a "stronghold"—an unmelted mountain, as it were—for those "who take refuge in him" (v. 7; cp. v. 5). But for His enemies—and here Nahum reversed the image from too little water to too much—God would appear as "an overwhelming flood" (v. 8).

The combination of images of too much and too little water was particularly suitable for Nineveh. The city was located in a region susceptible to hot desert winds, under which crops wither and life slows to a halt (cp. Jon. 4:8). But Nineveh was also bisected by a tributary of the Tigris River. Heavy winter rains periodically caused the river to overrun its banks and flood the city. Like other prophets, Nahum used images of known natural disasters to foreshadow the destruction of a people (cp. Joel 1:4–7; Amos 1:2–3; Mic. 1:4–5).

- *The Lord is good to those who take refuge in*
- *Him (1:7), but those who do not will meet*
- *God's wrath.*

A Call for Vengeance and Deliverance (vv. 9–15)

Nahum followed his hymn with a series of oracles announcing Nineveh's doom and the future salvation of Judah.

He began by chastising those who plot against the Lord (v. 9). As an example Nahum perhaps had in mind Sennacherib, the Assyrian king who had nearly conquered Jerusalem (v. 11). He likened such people to drunken men or thorns good only for the fire (v. 10; cp. Isa. 33:11–12).

The opening words of Nahum's hymn echo God's words to Moses the second time he climbed Mount Sinai to receive the tablets of the law. Moses had smashed the first tablets in anger when he descended the mountain and saw all Israel prostrating themselves before the golden calf (Exod. 32:15–20). God punished His people with a plague (Exod. 32:35) but then graciously renewed His covenant with them. Meeting Moses on the mountain a second time, God revealed Himself as one who is "merciful and gracious, slow to anger, and abounding in steadfast love and faithfulness" but who will by no means clear the guilty (Exod. 34:6–7, RSV).

Nahum then offered Judah a word of hope. Even though the Assyrians were a powerful people, they would fall before the hand of God (vv. 12–13). Judah had lived under the threat of Assyrian domination for more than one hundred years. But soon, Nahum prophesied, the Assyrian yoke of oppression would be broken so that Judah could live in peace.

"[Divine] anger is a reminder that man is in need of forgiveness, and that forgiveness must not be taken for granted." Abraham Heschel, *The Prophets*, vol. 2 (New York: Harper & Row, 1926), 65.

In the biblical world, news usually traveled by word of mouth. Messengers were sent to herald important announcements to a waiting populace (1 Sam. 31:9; 2 Chron. 30:6, 10; Esther 3:13–15; 8:13–14; Jer. 50:2). Often the oral message would be accompanied by a written proclamation. Jeremiah 51:31 describes a courier system whereby a series of messengers was able to carry news from the battlefield back to Babylon.

God commanded that Nineveh must fall, adding a sense of urgency to Nahum's prophecy (v. 14; cp. Isa. 34:16; Jer. 47:7). Nineveh's gods would also fall, signaling, according to the prevailing pagan theology of the day, the death of the city ("I will dig your grave!"). The result was that Nineveh's name would "be perpetuated no longer" (NKJV). After Nineveh fell in 612 B.C., the people of Assyria were gradually absorbed into other people groups and lost their identity.

Nahum finished in confidence with a vibrant message of hope (v. 15; cp. Isa. 52:7–10). Drawing on the imagery of a herald carrying news of a victory to an eager land (cp. Isa. 40:9), Nahum saw that Assyria's defeat would mean that life could return to normal for Judah. This it did for a while under the reign of Josiah (2 Kings 22:1–23:30; 2 Chron. 34:1–35:27). Centuries later the apostle Paul used Nahum's prophecy of a messenger bringing news of peace to describe the work of Christian missionaries carrying the gospel (lit. "good news") to a needy world (Rom. 10:14–17).

ℵ

- **The fall of Nineveh was sure, for God had**
- **commanded it. The people of Judah would**
- **have the freedom to worship God without fear**
- **of reprisal. This was indeed "good news."**

THE SIEGE AND FALL OF NINEVEH (2:1–3:19)

Having pronounced Nineveh's doom, Nahum went on to describe the battle that would lead to the fall of the city. After giving the reason for Nineveh's fall, Nahum concluded his book by declaring that Nineveh's defeat was inevitable.

The Battle for Nineveh (2:1–10)

In vivid language that fairly leaps off the page, Nahum rehearsed the siege (v. 1) and battle (vv. 3–10) that led to the fall of Nineveh. He described the scene in numerous short phrases, written in a staccato style that represents the quick "thrust and jab" of an ancient battle fought in close quarters. The horror of the ones being attacked is apparent (v. 10). Up to now it had been the Judeans who faced a violent death or captivity as Assyrians swarmed over the walls of their cities. Now the tide had turned, and from every indication Nahum relished the thought.

Nahum likened Nineveh's fate to a pool whose waters had run out on the ground (v. 8): once gone, the city's people and resources could never be brought back. Quite different was the future of "Jacob," God's own people of Israel and Judah (v. 2). Although likened to stripped vines, their "excellence" would be restored just as a new season brings leaves and fruit to a vine that looks dead. Nahum mentioned Israel's

Written records from ancient Babylon note that Nineveh fell in midsummer of the year 612 B.C., after a three-month siege. Archaeological evidence attests to the total and violent destruction of the city at this time. Nahum 2:6 appears to speak of sluice gates being opened upriver which flooded Nineveh, undercutting the foundations of the royal palace and causing it to collapse. While it is not possible to corroborate this specific event to the fall of Nineveh archaeologically, it is noteworthy that the ancient Greek historian Diodorus told how the river flooded and knocked down part of the wall of Nineveh, contributing to the city's defeat.

restoration (v. 2) before he described the destruction of Nineveh (vv. 3–10) in order to give it priority in the mind of his audience.

■ *Nineveh would fall in a terrible battle. The*
■ *horrors that the Assyrians had inflicted on*
■ *others would now fall on them. They would*
■ *get what they deserved, while God's favor*
■ *continued to rest on Judah.*

A Taunt over Nineveh's Destruction (2:11–13)

Having foreseen Nineveh's violent end, Nahum voiced a taunt against the doomed city. He compared the Assyrian capital to a den of lions, a fitting metaphor given Assyria's fascination with the king of beasts. The Assyrians had torn apart their prey and gorged themselves, as it were, on flesh (v. 12). They built a reputation on despoiling their victims, enriching themselves on the wealth of the world. Like a den of lions, the Assyrians feared no one and were feared by all.

The Assyrian general had publicly mocked Hezekiah when Sennacherib's army surrounded Jerusalem (2 Kings 18:17–35). Yet now it was Nahum who did the mocking: "Where are you *now?*" he asked the Assyrians (see v. 11).

It was not just Nahum who spoke against Nineveh, but God, "the LORD of hosts," as well (v. 13). "The LORD of hosts" is God's military title. His armies stood ready to overwhelm the Assyrian forces, devouring the young Assyrian "lions" and leaving them without prey.

Because of its strength and prowess, the lion was as revered in antiquity as it is today. Assyrian palaces were flanked with statues of winged lions. A popular motif in Assyrian reliefs showed the king on a lion hunt. In Assyrian religious texts Ishtar, the goddess of war, was portrayed as riding on or accompanied by a lion. Representations of lions appeared in Solomon's palace and Temple (1 Kings 7:29, 36; 10:19–20) and in the vision of Ezekiel's Temple (Ezek. 41:19). David's mighty men were described as having lion faces (1 Chron. 12:8), and God's voice and the voice of the king are likened to a lion's roar (Isa. 31:4; Hos. 11:10; Prov. 19:12).

N

- Nahum's "righteous taunt" echoed God's
- righteous anger against Nineveh. With "an
- eye for an eye" (cp. Exod. 21:23–25), the
- Assyrians were given the same treatment
- they had forced on others.

The Reason for Nineveh's Fall (3:1–7)

Nahum 3 opens with a woe oracle (vv. 1–7). Such oracles, or divine answers, typically gave the reasons persons were about to be punished by God (cp. Isa. 5:8–12, 18–23; 10:1–4; 29:1–4, 15–16; Mic. 2:1–11; Hab. 2:6–19; Zeph. 3:1–5). The prophets, feeling deeply the fate of the accused, began these oracles with the grievous cry "Woe!" (3:1).

Nahum's oracle included a short account of the battle for Nineveh (vv. 2–3; cp. 2:1–10). The sights, sounds, and smell of battle fairly leap off the page, suggesting that Nahum had personally experienced the horrors of war. The picture is intentionally shocking, to reinforce the frightfulness of Assyrian world domination. But now the Assyrians themselves would feel the horrors they had so cruelly inflicted on others.

Assyrian cruelty demanded that justice be served, but God was going to punish Nineveh for something far more serious than battlefield atrocities. Nahum explained that Nineveh was to be destroyed "because of the multitude of harlotries of the seductive harlot, . . . who sells nations through her harlotries, and families through her sorceries" (v. 4, NKJV). Biblical prophets typically used the image of a harlot to characterize Israel's covenant unfaithfulness toward God (Isa. 1:21; Jer. 2:20; 3:1–10; Ezek.

In the early part of the twentieth century a historian of ancient Assyria spoke of the "calculated frightfulness" of the Assyrian kings. Like the Nazis during World War II, the Assyrians mounted propaganda campaigns against their enemies in order to shock them into submission. Wall reliefs found in Nineveh portray a graphic record of Assyrian battle techniques. They show a variety of human tortures which the Assyrians inflicted on their conquered foes, including dismemberment, decapitation, and impaling.

16:1–63; Hos. 1:2–3:5; 4:15). This image was also appropriate for Nineveh, for by their power and wealth coupled with an overwhelming display of the Assyrian pagan worldview, they had seduced the Judeans to abandon the Lord for "superior" Assyrian ways (cp. 2 Kings 16:10–18).

Abominable Filth

The term *abominable filth* is used in the Bible to refer to a variety of idols and idolatrous practices (Deut. 29:17; 2 Kings 23:13, 24; Isa. 66:3; Jer. 4:1; 7:30; 13:27; 16:18; Ezek. 5:11; 11:21; 20:30). It also was used for the "abomination of desolation" which Daniel prophesied would be set up in the Temple (Dan. 11:31; cp. Matt. 24:15). The "abominable filth" which the nations would throw at Assyria in Nahum 3:6 was not idols but human waste. By using the term *abominable filth* in this way, Nahum showed the utter "filthiness" of Assyrian religious practices.

In defeat, Nineveh would be publicly humiliated. Their "nakedness" would be exposed like a prostitute in front of the nations, who would throw "abominable filth" upon her (vv. 5–6, NKJV). Unlike today, nakedness among the Hebrews did not carry connotations of embarrassment or sexual titillation. Rather, nakedness indicated shame for sin (cp. Gen. 9:20–23; Isa. 3:17; 20:1–6; 47:2–3; Jer. 13:22–27). Totally depraved, Nineveh would lie in disgrace, abandoned and unmourned at death (v. 7).

■ *The prophets were always careful to state*
■ *that sin lies at the root of all human prob-*
■ *lems. While Assyria's enemies saw brutal*
■ *cruelty, Nahum peered deeper, into the*
■ *Assyrian heart. The Assyrians were pun-*
■ *ished for who they were inside, and, once*
■ *exposed, their fate caused the nations to*
■ *recoil.*

The Inevitability of Nineveh's Fall (3:8–19)

To seal the case for Nineveh's destruction, Nahum reminded his audience of the fall of No-Amon (Thebes) (v. 8). In spite of its strength, No-Amon fell to Ashurbanipal in 663 B.C., as the Assyrians pushed deep into Egypt to seize the treasures of the Nile. Egypt and its allies—Ethiopia, Put, and Lubim (the latter two were probably part of modern Libya)—were no match for the Assyrian might (v. 9), and the people of No-Amon were killed or taken away in chains (v. 10).

The defeat of No-Amon fulfilled a centuries-long Assyrian dream to conquer Egypt. It was therefore appropriate that Nahum used this, Assyria's crowning victory, to speak of the inevitable fall of Nineveh. When their capital fell, the Assyrians would be as dazed men, drunkenly stumbling for cover from the enemy (v. 11).

Nahum used several metaphors to describe Nineveh's precarious position: the city was like ripe figs about to fall from a tree (v. 12); its soldiers were "women" (v. 13)—an insult, given the ancient Near Eastern context—and the gateways to its land already lay open (v. 13). Nahum dared the Assyrians to prepare for siege (v. 14), for their destruction was inevitable (v. 15). Finally, Nahum likened the Assyrians to locust: while destructive in their day (cp. Judg. 6:5; Joel 1:4; 2:25; Rev. 9:3, 7), locust disappear as quickly as they come, to the regret of no one (vv. 15–17). Finally, the Assyrian leaders were but sleeping shepherds whose people, like sheep scattered on the mountains, were lost and helpless (v. 18).

It was not just for Judah's sake that Assyria was about to fall. The entire ancient world had cowered under Assyrian might and suffered under their heavy hand of evil (v. 19). Destruction would come. It was inevitable. And there was no staying the hand of God.

The book of Nahum is one of the few prophetic books that does not end on an upbeat note. For Judah, however, Nineveh's destruction *was*

No-Amon ("the city of the god Amon") was the Egyptian name for a city in Upper Egypt which is better known as Thebes (Jer. 46:25; Ezek. 30:14–16; Nah. 3:8). It was located where the modern cities of Karnak and Luxor now lie. Thebes reached the height of its splendor during the Egyptian New Kingdom (the sixteenth through twelfth centuries B.C.), when the temples of Karnak, Luxor, Deir el-bahri and Medinet Habu, now popular with tourists, were built.

good news. God was about to punish evil—evil that had been directed against Judah for many years. Judah would be freed from foreign domination, and under Josiah, experience national and religious revival (2 Kings 22:1–23:27). But an insightful reader recognizes that God's standards are even more exacting for His own covenant people. It is *they* who have the greater responsibility for doing what He requires. The warning was implicit: Judah, too, could fall under divine wrath. But for now, Nahum and his contemporaries saw a day when their nation would be vindicated and they could again live in peace.

N

- *Nineveh faced certain destruction. God's*
- *wrath is His eternal opposition to evil. It is*
- *not at all in conflict with His love. What kind*
- *of love permits evil to flourish indefinitely?*

QUESTIONS TO GUIDE YOUR STUDY

1. How does Nahum's hymn (1:1–8) help us to interpret his book?
2. The books of Jonah and Nahum both speak about judgment against Nineveh. How are they different? Why?
3. Was it important for ancient Israel that an entire book of the Bible be devoted to the destruction of Assyria? Why is the message of Nahum important for Christians?

THE BOOK OF HABAKKUK

The Hebrew word that describes Habakkuk's prophecy in 1:1 is translated "oracle" by the NIV and RSV and "burden" by the NKJV. An oracle is an answer given by God to a difficult question, and certainly this describes the content of the book. The word *burden*, a more literal translation of the Hebrew word, better conveys the sense of the book. *Burden* was probably a technical term for a specific kind of oracle. It is used in the Old Testament to introduce prophetic threats, messages that were hard for the prophet's audience to bear and no doubt difficult for the prophet to deliver.

Unlike most of the other prophetic books, Habakkuk does not record the public sermons or pronouncements of God's prophets. Rather, it contains two private conversations between Habakkuk and God in which Habakkuk questioned God's willingness to help His people. These are followed by a prayer in which Habakkuk came to terms with God's answers. We are able to "eavesdrop" on these conversations because they are recorded for us in the Bible. By doing so, we learn how to respond when God appears not to answer our questions, either.

A DISCOURSE WITH GOD ABOUT INJUSTICE IN JUDAH (1:1–11)

Institutionalized injustice ran rampant in Judah. God allowed it to continue but then announced that He would use the Babylonians to punish Judah.

Habakkuk's Cry: "Why Is There So Much Injustice in Judah?" (vv. 1–4)

Habakkuk ministered in Judah at the very end of the seventh century B.C. The Assyrians were no longer a threat (Nineveh had fallen in 612 B.C.), and under King Josiah (640–609 B.C.), Judah had experienced a national and religious revival (cp. 2 Kings 22:1–23:30). The effects of this revival, however, failed to penetrate deeply into Judean society, and under Josiah's successors, the nation again turned away from God (cp. 2 Kings 23:31–24:20). The destruction of Judah and Jerusalem by Babylon was imminent.

The tenor of the first four verses of Habakkuk betrays a frustrated man. Habakkuk knew what it was to be righteous but saw very little righteousness in Judean society. He had been crying to God for a long time and was weary of not being answered (v. 2). The problem was quite personal; Habakkuk himself had suffered "plundering and violence" (v. 3, NKJV). He and others who tried to follow God's ways were victims of their fellowmen, violated by a judicial system that intentionally favored the wicked (v. 4). God's laws (*Torah*)—various instructions for life handed down to Moses and preserved in the books of Exodus, Leviticus, and Deuteronomy—were intended to foster a peaceful, well-ordered, and prosperous society. In Habakkuk's day these laws were not followed, and as a result basic issues of justice were ignored.

The cry of the righteous sufferer was voiced often in the Old Testament but perhaps no more eloquently than by Job. God allowed Satan to attack Job's wealth, his family, and finally his own health. Job's wife counseled her troubled and bewildered husband: "Curse God and die!" (Job 2:9), but Job refused to do so. Job's suffering grew worse when he realized that the violence and lack of justice he was experiencing were due not to other people but God (Job 19:5–12). Nevertheless, Job remained faithful, and God restored him to favor in due time (Job 38:1–42:17).

- God's own prophet became a victim of insti-
- tutionalized unrighteousness within Judah.
- Habakkuk cried repeatedly to God but found
- no satisfaction. What else was he to do?

God's Response: "Judah Will Be Punished" (vv. 5–11)

God finally did answer but in a most unexpected way. Habakkuk could not believe what was about to happen (v. 5). God was going to use the Chaldeans, a "bitter and hasty nation" (v. 6, NKJV), to punish Judah. The Chaldeans are better known to world history as the Babylonians.

God described the Babylonians to Habakkuk in a way that must have reminded the prophet of the dreaded Assyrians. Babylonian military power was unrelenting (v. 8), and no king or fortified city could stand in their way (vv. 9–10). What was worse, the Babylonians were bringing "violence," the very evil that God was supposed to be purging from Judah (v. 9; cp. 1:2–3).

The Babylonians were God's instrument to punish Judah, much like Cyrus, the pagan king of Persia, would be God's instrument to bring Judah back to their homeland (cp. Isa. 45:1). Although used by God, the Babylonians made no pretext of recognizing His divine hand in world affairs. The Babylonians' "justice and dignity proceed from themselves," God reminded Habakkuk, and their "own might is their god" (vv. 7, 11, NKJV).

On his first missionary journey the apostle Paul preached a sermon in the synagogue of Pisidian Antioch. As his conclusion, he used Habakkuk 1:5 to warn the Jews what might happen if they rejected the message of Jesus (Acts 13:40–41). Many believed, and the entire city gathered to hear Paul preach the next Sabbath (Acts 13:42–44).

"Look at the nations and watch—and be utterly amazed. For I am going to do something in your days that you would not believe, even if you were told" (Hab. 1:5).

The Chaldeans were an ancient people group whose homeland lay in the marshlands where the Tigris and Euphrates rivers flow into the Persian Gulf.

71

There was nothing in God's answer that could cause Habakkuk comfort. God was sending the Babylonians to punish Judah, and Judah would have to endure even greater wickedness and violence as a result. Now what was Habakkuk to do?

The phrase "they heap up earth and take it" in 1:10 (RSV) refers to siege ramps, a technique of offensive warfare used by the Assyrians, the Babylonians, and the Romans. Dramatic archaeological evidence of ancient siege ramps can be seen in Israel at Lachish, which was conquered by the Assyrians in 701 B.C., and Masada, overrun by the Romans in A.D. 73.

A DISCOURSE WITH GOD ABOUT INJUSTICE AGAINST JUDAH (1:12–2:20)

Habakkuk complained that God's answer was unfair. God replied that the Babylonians, too, would be punished for their evil ways. In the meantime Habakkuk must remain faithful and wait.

Habakkuk's Cry: "But Why Must Judah Be Punished by the Babylonians?" (1:12–17)

God was going to use Babylon to chastise Judah. Habakkuk's initial reaction was to trust God's judgment (v. 12). God was, after all, "from everlasting" and ought to know what was best for His people. In acknowledging this, Habakkuk showed that he was familiar with the message of Job, another righteous sufferer. In the great theophany at the end of the book of Job, God showed that as Creator He reserved the right to do whatever He wanted to with His people (Job 38:1–41:34).

But then Habakkuk challenged God. He reminded God that He was too pure even to look at evil; why then would He use "those who deal treacherously" in order to punish one "more righteous than he" (v. 13, NKJV)? The Babylonians were going to overrun all of Judah—the righteous and wicked alike. It was one thing for Judeans to victimize other Judeans (cp. 1:2–4); it was quite another for Babylonians, who had no thought of God's ways, to be invited to do the same. How could God silently condone such blatant injustice (v. 13)?

Habakkuk compared the Judeans to fish in the sea and the Babylonians to fishermen with hooks and great nets, eagerly harvesting whatever they pulled up and then returning for more (vv. 14–17). The Babylonians "sacrificed to their net" (v. 16), worshiping their own strength and the things that made them successful. In the prevailing theology of the day, a nation's god was considered superior to another if his armies conquered those of his rival. Wouldn't the nations think that God approved of the Babylonians' behavior if He let them conquer Judah?

- *Habakkuk knew what he was supposed to*
- *believe but had a hard time doing so when his*
- *belief system ran into the hard realities of*
- *life. Why do God's people suffer at the hands*
- *of the wicked? Why do the unrighteous pros-*
- *per at the expense of the righteous? For*
- *Habakkuk, these questions demanded an*
- *answer.*

God's Response: "Just Remain Faithful and Wait" (2:1–5)

Rather than give up on God or challenge His wisdom in human affairs, Habakkuk decided to wait and see what God would say about his complaint (v. 1). That Habakkuk chose to wait, like a lone sentinel upon a watchtower, shows not only that he was persistent but that he still believed in the sovereignty of God.

Waiting for God to answer prayer is one of the most difficult tasks Christians face. The saints of the Bible often waited for God, agonizing over their circumstances in the meantime. The most poignant cries for divine action are found in the book of Psalms. Sometimes the psalmist accused God of hiding His face even though His people had done nothing wrong (e.g., Ps. 27:7–9). The psalmists counsel their readers to wait for God with confidence, knowing He will answer in the end (Ps. 27:14).

The Hebrew word translated "faith" in Habakkuk 2:4 means "faithfulness," "steadfastness," or "trustworthiness." It implies a continued state of being, a deliberate and conscientious effort to walk in God's ways. It also includes the ideas of belief and trust which are more common to the New Testament concept of faith. Quoting this verse three times, the writers of the New Testament recognized that saving faith was faith that believed in God but also resulted in faithful living (Rom. 1:17; Gal. 3:11; Heb. 10:37–38).

When God finally did speak, He made sure that not only Habakkuk, but also anyone else who cared, would know what His answer was. Habakkuk was told to write down God's answer plainly, on tablets, so that "he may run who reads it" (v. 2, RSV). The reference to running is twofold. Such tablets were carried by heralds throughout the land for quick public dissemination (cp. 1 Sam. 31:9; 2 Sam. 18:19; 2 Chron. 30:6; Esther 3:13–15; Isa. 8:1; Jer. 50:2; Nah. 1:15). More importantly, the ones who read the tablets and heeded God's answer would not only be able to "walk humbly with your God" (Mic. 6:8) but "run" with Him (cp. Isa. 40:31).

God told Habakkuk that His people must remain faithful in spite of their prolonged trials (vv. 3–4). All of the Old Testament saints waited for the fulfillment of divine promises (Heb. 11:13; cp. Gen. 15:1–6), and Habakkuk was no exception. The righteous ones—those who were faithful to God—would live. The rest would be consumed by the insatiable appetite of death (2:5).

- *Waiting and remaining faithful are hard to*
- *do, but this is exactly what God prescribed*
- *for Habakkuk. He requires no less from us*
- *today.*

Woe Oracles Against Babylon (2:6–20)

Having received his answer, Habakkuk proceeded to pronounce five "taunting riddles" against those who opposed the ways of God. Because each begins with the word "Woe!" (Heb. *hoy*; 2:6, 9, 12, 15, 19; cp. Mic. 2:1), Bible interpreters usually call these "woe oracles." Habakkuk did not specifically say that they were aimed at the Babylonians, only that they were spoken by "all these" against "him" (v. 6, RSV). The pronouns are intentionally unspecific. While the Babylonians were the primary referent, Habakkuk wanted to include his own people in the judgment should they, too, continue to persist in "destruction and violence" (cp. 1:2–4, RSV). In God's eyes, sinners are all the same.

These five woe oracles provide a look at the social injustices of Habakkuk's day. Each contained a reversal of fortunes, a common prophetic theme (Mic. 2:2–5; Nah. 3:8–15; cp. 1 Sam. 2:5–8; Matt. 19:30):

- The first oracle was aimed at people who took and used for themselves things that belonged to others (vv. 6–8). Those who borrow heavily must eventually face their debtors. Habakkuk likened wealth which is gained by irresponsible borrowing to riches that are plundered through warfare. Both are dishonest gain, tantamount to taking "what is not one's own."

- The second oracle addressed persons or nations who attempted to secure their own positions by exploiting others (vv. 9–11). Habakkuk likened security to a home built high on a rock, safely out of harm's way (cp. Obad. 3–4). If the builder used "evil gain" to construct his house, he would forfeit his own life.

- The third oracle addressed those who built cities through violence and oppression, or who allowed communities to suffer under injustice (vv. 12–14). Such efforts are "in vain" and worthy of nothing but the fire. In sharp contrast Habakkuk

The social and economic difficulties which came as a result of heavy borrowing were anticipated by the Mosaic Law, which commanded that fellow Israelites should not be charged interest on loans (Exod. 22:25; Deut. 23:19–20; cp. Neh. 5:7–12; Luke 6:34). The apostle Paul taught that it is better not to owe anyone anything (Rom. 13:8). Nevertheless, the Bible recognizes that some loans are necessary and counsels against unjust interest rates (Ps. 15:5; Prov. 28:8; Ezek. 18:8, 13). Those who borrow and do not repay are called "wicked" (Ps. 37:21). Because spiritual wealth is a far greater resource than financial wealth, the Bible cautions against misplaced efforts in acquiring riches (Prov. 23:4–5; Luke 12:16–21; 1 Tim. 6:9–10; Heb. 13:5–6).

compared God's glorious kingdom to the overpowering force of the earth's oceans. Coming at the midpoint of the woe oracles, verse 14 serves to draw the reader back to the promised blessings of God.

- The fourth oracle speaks of drunkenness (vv. 15–17). Drunkenness was usually condemned by biblical writers as a gross indulgence practiced by the wealthy, and as such Habakkuk listed it with other injustices of exploitation. In response, God would pour His cup of wrath upon those who took advantage of others by stripping them of their dignity and robbing them of their ability to act with sober judgment (cp. Jer. 25:15, 27).

- The fifth oracle poked fun at idolatry (vv. 18–19). Habakkuk exposed the folly of idolatry by describing the process by which an idol was made (cp. Isa. 40:18–20). It was impossible for man-made images to provide any sort of revelation from God, and hence those who looked to them for guidance, be they Babylonians or Judeans, were without hope.

Habakkuk ended his woe oracles with one of the most majestic verses in all of the books of the Minor Prophets: "But the LORD is in His holy temple. Let all the earth keep silence before Him" (v. 20, NKJV). This affirmation stands in sharp contrast to the silent idols of the previous oracle and provides a fitting conclusion for all five. In the face of the chaos of the nations and the destructive violence running rampant in Judah, Habakkuk called for all the earth to "sit down and shut up" in the presence of God. Our only response to God's work—or to His waiting to work—should be submission before Him (cp. Zeph. 1:7).

- *In his woe oracles, Habakkuk attacked vio-*
- *lence and destruction wherever he saw it,*
- *whether in Babylon or Judah. He called for*
- *all people to submit to God's will—hard*
- *advice for those used to getting their own*
- *way.*

A PRAYER OF RECONCILIATION (3:1–19)

Habakkuk ended his book with a magnificent prayer declaring the universal sovereignty of God. Overcome with the power of God's presence, he resolved to wait for God to act even though he would suffer great personal loss in the meantime.

Two Theophanies (vv. 1–15)

Habakkuk began his prayer by describing two spectacular theophanies, or appearances of God in physical form. In these theophanies he described God using language and literary forms typical to the book of Psalms. For this reason, and because Habakkuk's prayer begins with a superscription similar to those found throughout the book of Psalms (3:1; cp. Ps. 5:1, etc.), many Bible interpreters suggest that Habakkuk's prayer was (or became) a psalm used in Israelite worship.

Habakkuk opened his prayer by acknowledging that he knew that God had intervened on behalf of Israel in the past. Knowing God's character, Habakkuk asked that in his own day, an age of wrath, God would again visit His people in a mighty way (v. 2).

Shigionoth

The superscription of Habakkuk's prayer contains the notation "according to Shigionoth." The word *Shigionoth* is an untranslated Hebrew word that may indicate the tone or mood in which his prayer was intended to be sung in ancient Israelite Temple worship. If so, it is analogous to terms such as *andante* or *moderato* which are often found at the beginning of written musical compositions today. The exact meaning of Shigionoth is unknown. Habakkuk's prayer ends with other notations to the choirmaster (3:19). Similar musical terms appear in various biblical psalms and are sometimes translated into English (e.g. Ps. 5:1; 6:1; 7:1; 45:1, etc.).

The four places mentioned in Habakkuk 3:3, 7 are all in the wilderness through which Moses led the people of Israel on their journey from Egypt to Canaan. Teman was a desert oasis in mountainous Edom (Seir), southeast of Judah (Obad. 9; cp. Deut. 33:2). Mount Paran may be another name for Mount Sinai, locating it within the great wilderness of Paran, a rugged and desolate area of eastern Sinai (cp. Num. 10:12; 13:3). Cushan is connected in Habakkuk 3:7 with Midian, the vast mountainous desert region of the northwestern Arabian peninsula. Moses married a woman whom the Bible identified as both a Midianite and a Cushite (Exod. 2:16–22; Num. 12:1). Cush is usually thought to have been in Egypt or Ethiopia (Ezek. 29:10), but its exact location is unknown.

The first theophany, set in the vast desert wilderness, portrayed God's appearance at Mount Sinai (vv. 2–7). God burst forth as a flashing light that filled the entire earth (vv. 3–4). Many interpreters take this to be a lightning storm (cp. Exod. 19:16); but based on a similar theophany described poetically in Deuteronomy 33:2, it may be better understood as a brilliant sunrise over the eastern mountains of Teman. Habakkuk also pictured God as a mighty king accompanied by a retinue that included "pestilence" and "plague," His agents to wreck havoc on the earth (v. 5). When God comes, it is as if the "eternal mountains"—including the granite massif of Sinai—are scattered (v. 6, RSV; cp. Judg. 5:3–5; Mic. 1:3–4), and the tents of the desert dwellers in Cushan and Midian tremble on the unstable ground (v. 7).

The second theophany was set over the sea and its coastlands (vv. 8–15). The language is that of a powerful storm, churning the deep and terrorizing anything that tries to venture upon the sea. God appeared as a mighty warrior with horse and chariot (vv. 8, 15), arrows and spear (vv. 9, 11). He defeated the enemy in the midst of raging waters much as He had brought salvation to Israel when Moses parted the Red Sea (vv. 12–13; cp. Exod. 15:1–18).

These two theophanies answered Habakkuk's prior questions as to why God appeared to allow evil to go unchecked. God's answer was not specific, but it was unassailable. Habakkuk was called to understand exactly who God was (and, is), and submit his daily troubles, whatever they were, to Him. Job had been given the same answer after he, too, challenged God's goodness and power (Job 38:1–41:34).

N

- God showed Himself to Habakkuk as the
- absolute sovereign of the world. Except by
- God's grace, nothing can stand before Him.
- He easily overcomes human troubles, even
- those caused by a force as formidable as the
- Babylonians.

Habakkuk's Quiet Confidence in God (vv. 16–19)

Like Job, Habakkuk responded the only way he could—in quiet submission and trust (v. 16; cp. Job 42:1–6). His insides trembled, both at the overwhelming presence of God (cp. Dan. 10:2–9) and at the prospect of having to endure an invasion by the Babylonians. All he could do was accept God's will for His people and wait for the divine wrath to pass.

Habakkuk ended his prayer—and his book—with one of the strongest statements of confidence found in the entire Bible. Centuries before, Moses had warned Israel what would happen if God withheld His blessing from their land: crops would fail, livestock would be barren, and the land would become as unproductive as the desert (Deut. 28:15–24). Because of Judah's sins (cp. 1:2–4), God's curse became reality in Habakkuk's day (v. 17). Even so, Habakkuk declared that he would not only endure the trouble but also rejoice in the face of it (v. 18). God was both his salvation and his strength and would allow him to triumph in the end (v. 19).

Habakkuk likened himself to a hind (probably a red deer), treading nimbly along rocky cliffs far above harm's way (v. 19). This verse is also found in Psalm 18:33 and 2 Samuel 22:34. According to its superscription, Psalm 18 was written after the Lord had delivered David from all of his enemies. The psalm presents David as a mighty and successful warrior, triumphant over his many foes. Habakkuk drew on the life of David to express his confidence in God's ability to see him through whatever troubles lay ahead.

- *Habakkuk remained faithful in spite of the*
- *trying circumstances of his life. His confi-*
- *dence in God was unshakable. Having sub-*
- *mitted to the sovereignty of God, he was able*
- *to triumph in the face of tragedy. The apostle*
- *Paul said the same: "I can do all things in*
- *him who strengthens me" (Phil. 4:13, RSV).*

QUESTIONS TO GUIDE YOUR STUDY

1. How do Habakkuk's dialogues with God provide a model for prayer today?
2. How can God's love for His people be reconciled with the prevalence of sin in the world?
3. How can we live a life of faith in the midst of chaos?

THE BOOK OF ZEPHANIAH

STUDY OUTLINE

The book of Zephaniah sounds a no-holds-barred call for judgment against Judah. Little outlet is given for repentance, although, as with most of the other prophetic books, Zephaniah ends with a glorious picture of restoration. Although the overall message is stern, the poetry carrying the message is beautiful and worthy of careful reading.

THE DAY OF THE LORD AS A DAY OF JUDGMENT (1:1–3:8)

Zephaniah warned Judah that God's judgment would fall soon on them and on their neighbors. God was going to "make a sudden end of all who live in the earth" (1:18).

The Coming Day of the Lord (1:1–2:3)

Zephaniah announced that the nation of Judah would be destroyed at the coming day of the Lord.

"Stretching out one's hand" toward someone or something symbolized royal authority. The Persian King Ahasuerus allowed guests into his throne room only when he held out his royal scepter; not even his queen was exempt from this protocol (Esther 5:1–2). By stretching out his hand against Judah, God announced His sovereign right to do with His people whatever He wished (1:4). The writer of 2 Kings spoke of God's stretching out a measuring line over Judah by which He gauged its peoples' righteousness (2 Kings 21:13).

An Announcement of Universal Judgment (1:1–6)

Zephaniah prophesied during the reign of Josiah, the last godly king of Judah (v. 1). His book predates Habakkuk by about two decades, and the issues facing each prophet were essentially the same. Within a generation Judah would be destroyed by the Babylonians and Jerusalem, God's chosen city, would be burned. Zephaniah's genealogy (v. 1) covered four generations, linking the prophet to Hezekiah. This was probably the same Hezekiah who, as king of Judah, successfully faced the Assyrian threat of 701 B.C. (cp. 2 Kings 18:13–19:37). Jerusalem was spared destruction by the Assyrians in Hezekiah's day only because of the king's faithfulness. With Hezekiah as an ancestor, Zephaniah was well qualified to provide political and religious commentary on Judah during the troubled days of the late seventh century B.C.

Zephaniah opened his book with a divine announcement of the sudden and complete destruction of the earth (v. 2). The language is reminiscent of God's announcement to Noah that, because of human wickedness, he would "blot out mankind . . . from the face of the ground" (Gen. 6:7, RSV). The things to be "swept away," and the order in which they were mentioned, is significant: first men, then beasts, birds, and fish (v. 3; cp. Gen. 6:7). This reverses the order of the same categories of beings created by God during the seven days of Creation (Gen. 1:20, 24, 26). Zephaniah's intent was to announce that a wholly different kind of day was coming, a day of *de-Creation*, in which God would cleanse the earth of its wickedness.

The specific kind of wickedness mentioned by Zephaniah was not social or economic injustice (as was condemned by Micah and Habakkuk) but a breach of God's covenant. Judah had forsaken the Lord and His ways for the gods and ways of the Canaanites (vv. 4–6). God demanded unconditional loyalty from His people. Throughout the monarchy the people of Israel and Judah had divided their religious loyalties between the Lord and various Canaanite deities, and the latter usually came out on top. Several Judean kings, including Josiah, strove to purify Judean worship (cp. 1 Kings 15:12–13; 2 Kings 12:4–16; 22:3–23:25; 2 Chron. 29:1–31:21; 34:1–35:19). Zephaniah spoke to the need of Josiah's reforms but recognized that these reforms would not reach the heart and soul of his people.

- *Zephaniah pictured the destruction of Judah*
- *as if the entire earth were being de-created.*
- *The root cause of its destruction was spiritual apostasy against the Lord.*

A Description of the Day of the Lord (1:7–2:3)

Zephaniah called the period of judgment that was coming upon Judah and the nations "the day of the LORD" (1:7, 14) or "the day of the wrath of the LORD" (1:18; 2:2, 3, RSV). Biblical writers used these terms to refer to any period of time that was totally monopolized by the Lord to expedite His judgment on the earth (cp. Isa. 13:9; Joel 1:15; 2:28–32; Amos 5:18, etc.). For Zephaniah, this meant that Jerusalem would be destroyed by the Babylonians and the Judean monarchy would cease to exist.

The most familiar "day of the Lord" passage in the Bible is found in Joel 2:28–32. Joel spoke of a day when God would pour out His Spirit on all flesh; this was fulfilled at the day of Pentecost (Joel 2:28–29; cp. Acts 2:14–18). He also spoke of a day when great portents would appear in the in the sky (Joel 2:30–32). The fulfillment of this portion of the prophecy was anticipated in Acts 2:19–21, but its final fulfillment will not be realized until the Second Coming of Christ (Rev. 6:1–9:21).

The phrase "every one who leaps over the threshold" (1:9, RSV) is difficult to understand and may refer to ancient pagan religious fetishes (cp. 1 Sam. 5:4–5).

Zephaniah 1:10–11 attests to the prophet's intimate knowledge of the topography of his city. Like the old city of Jerusalem today, Zephaniah's Jerusalem was built on and around several hills. The city's Fish Gate was located near the northwest corner of the Temple mount, and the second quarter encompassed a higher hill within the city to the west. The "Mortar" (NASB) or "Maktesh" (NKJV) was the valley between the two where the merchants and traders congregated. The entire city was ringed by higher hills. The unique topography of Jerusalem, accurately described in Zephaniah 1:10–11, allowed a loud cry to echo around the city and reverberate through its valleys, sending an alarm to all the inhabitants.

Zephaniah first called the nations to "be silent!" before God (1:7), for only by doing so would they acknowledge their powerlessness before Him. His cry echoes Habakkuk's call for silence amid the violence and chaos running rampant on the earth (Hab. 2:20). God was preparing a blood sacrifice, and Judah's leaders and crown prince were the sacrificial victims (1:7–8). Like Habakkuk, Zephaniah attacked violence and fraud (1:9), the social outworking of religious apostasy.

When the day of the Lord arrived, the cry of judgment would echo off of the hills and sound throughout the residential quarters of Jerusalem (1:10–11). God was personally going to search out the inhabitants of the city who thought He was no longer active in society (1:12). Although such people had planned lives of ease, they would not enjoy the fruit of their labors (1:13; cp. Deut. 28:30–31).

Zephaniah spoke with a sharp sense of urgency. The day of the Lord was "near and hastening fast," bringing with it the darkness and gloom that attends a horrible defeat in battle (1:14–16, RSV). Zephaniah's reference to "clouds and thick darkness" echoes the awe-filled appearance of God at Mount Sinai (cp. Exod. 19:16; 20:21; Deut. 4:11); with this reference, Zephaniah taught that the very same God who had brought His covenant to Israel was now removing His people from His presence. As a result, they would be blind, weak, and poor, easily consumed by God's fiery wrath (1:17–18).

Zephaniah called the people to come together one last time to seek the Lord (2:1–3). Although he offered no promises, he held out hope that those who truly sought after righteousness and humility might be spared the wrath to come.

- *The terrible day of the Lord, a day of God's*
- *undiluted wrath, was coming fast to Judah*
- *and Jerusalem. Zephaniah held little hope of*
- *escape, even for those who remained faithful*
- *to God. Generations of sinful living had so*
- *polluted society that everyone alike was*
- *affected.*

Specific Oracles of Judgment (2:4–3:8)

Zephaniah prophesied that God would destroy Judah's enemies: the Philistines, Moabites, Ammonites, Ethiopians (Egyptians), and Assyrians. Jerusalem, too, would be judged, but God would enable its surviving remnant to possess their enemies' lands.

Judgment on the Nations (2:4–15)

The Philistines had inhabited the Mediterranean seacoast on the western edge of Judah's tribal inheritance for as long as the Judeans had been in their land. For centuries the Philistines had been Judah's nemesis to the west, encroaching onto their land and cutting off Judah's access to the sea (e.g., Judg. 13:1–16:31; 1 Sam. 4:1–7:14; 13:1–14:52; 17:1–58; 2 Sam. 5:17–25; 2 Chron. 26:6–7; 28:18). Zephaniah announced that the major Philistine cities—Gaza, Ashkelon, Ashdod, and Ekron—would all fall on the day of the Lord (vv. 3–4). More importantly, the Philistine's land would be possessed by "the remnant of the house of Judah," and God would "restore [the] fortunes" of His people (v. 7). These phrases anticipate the more detailed description of Judah's restoration in chapter 3.

The Philistine confederation was organized around five cities: Gaza, Ashkelon, Ashdod, Ekron, and Gath (cp. 1 Sam. 6:4, 17). Archaeological evidence suggests that ancient Gath (Tell es-Safi) was destroyed in the mid-eighth century B.C. This coincides with an attack on the city by Judah's King Uzziah described in 2 Chronicles 26:6. Biblical and Assyrian records listing the Philistine cities from about the middle of the eighth century B.C. on, fail to mention Gath, further corroborating Uzziah's destruction of the city (e.g. Jer. 25:20; Amos 1:6–8; Zeph. 2:4; Zech. 9:5–7).

The Cherethites (2:5) were a tribe or clan of Philistines. Their land bordered southern Judah (1 Sam. 30:14). Cherethites served as mercenaries in David's army (2 Sam. 8:18; 15:18; 23:22–23) and assisted at Solomon's coronation (1 Kings 1:38, 44).

The Moabites and Ammonites, Judah's neighbors in Transjordan to the east, were to be judged for their haughty attitude toward Judah (v. 8, 10; cp. Obad. 3–4, 11–12). Zephaniah had no specific act in view but rather a history of political and religious tensions between his nation and theirs (cp. Judg. 3:12–30; 11:4–33; 1 Kings 11:7–8; 2 Kings 3:4–27; 13:20; 2 Chron. 20:1–23; 2 Chron. 26:8; etc.). Moab and Ammon would become like the arid wasteland around the Dead Sea, the body of water that separated Judah from its eastern neighbors (v. 9). Their lands, like that of the Philistines, would be plundered and possessed by Judah (v. 9).

Casting his eyes to the distant southern and northern horizons, Zephaniah announced that God would also destroy the "Ethiopians" and Assyrians (vv. 12–13). Because Ethiopian (or Cushite) dynasties had ruled over Egypt from time to time up to Zephaniah's day, it can be assumed that he had in mind Egypt rather than peoples from the area of present-day Ethiopia. Egypt and Assyria were the superpowers of the seventh century B.C.

Zephaniah's prophecy against Ethiopia (Egypt) was brief (v. 12). He did not foresee Egypt's total destruction; and, in fact, Egypt survived for centuries as an important nation in the ancient Near East.

The Assyrians and their capital city of Nineveh, on the other hand, received more attention by Zephaniah. Like Nahum, Zephaniah foresaw Assyria's total destruction (v. 13). The city of Nineveh, once the wonder of the ancient world, was to become home only to the wild beasts (vv. 14–15). To the regret of no one in Judah, Nineveh was destroyed in 612 B.C. and ceased to exist as an Assyrian city (cp. Nah. 3:19).

N

- **Judah's enemies both great and small were going to be destroyed by the hand of God.**
- **Zephaniah hinted that the Judeans would possess the lands of their neighbors. This provided some measure of comfort as their own judgment loomed before them.**

Judgment on Jerusalem (3:1–5)

Zephaniah again turned his anger against Jerusalem. His pronouncement of judgment was based on Judah's haughty attitude and actions. Like their neighbors, the people of Jerusalem had trusted in their own wisdom and strength. Having ignored God's counsel, they became just another "oppressing city" (vv. 1–2, RSV; cp. Hab. 1:2–4).

Zephaniah reserved special words of judgment for Jerusalem's leaders: the civil officials, the judges, the prophets, and the priests (vv. 3–4). All were doing exactly the opposite of what they were commissioned to do. For instance, rather than caring for their people, the officials and judges were ravenous animals, preying on others to satisfy their own desires (cp. Jer. 5:26–29; Ezek. 34:2–6; Mic. 3:1–3). The prophets had been called faithfully to deliver God's word but instead were "wanton [and] faithless" (cp. Mic. 3:5–7). The priests of Jerusalem "polluted the sanctuary" and did "violence" (or violation) to God's law. Without proper leadership, it is no wonder Jerusalem had become a "rebellious and oppressing city" (v. 1).

Zephaniah's use of "evening wolves" (3:3; cp. Hab. 1:8) to describe Judah's judges was particularly sinister. Wolves habitually lay low throughout the day until dusk, striking when other animals are tired and ready to bed down for the night. They usually descend in packs, tearing their prey and gorging themselves on flesh. Jesus described false prophets as "ravenous wolves" (Matt. 7:15, RSV), and the apostle Paul referred to false teachers as "fierce wolves" not sparing the flock (Acts 20:29).

In the midst of the oppressing city, the Lord continued faithfully to show His righteousness day after day (v. 5). It was only by His grace that the people of Jerusalem could survive the day of the Lord and be restored to their land (cp. 3:9–20).

- *Zephaniah's prophecy of judgment reached*
- *its climax with his description of the corrupt*
- *leadership of Jerusalem. But the Lord*
- *remained righteous, providing a ray of hope*
- *for His beleaguered people.*

Judgment on the Nations (3:6–8)

Zephaniah ended his prophecy of judgment by again turning against the nations. This time he spoke of the past: "I (i.e., God) have cut off nations; . . . I have laid waste their streets . . .; their cities have been made desolate" (v. 6, RSV). Because no specific nations are mentioned, it is clear that Zephaniah intended Judah to view the sweep of their history and recall the rise and fall of many dynasties. Why should Judah think *they* were the exception to this rule, the only nation that would never fall?

Previous biblical history should have taught the people of Judah that God orchestrates the fall of nations (e.g., Deut. 9:4–5; 2 Kings 17:1–18). Judah had been given plenty of examples from which to learn how to live. Therefore God's conclusion, "Surely, then, they will fear me," is tinged with expectation but also sarcasm (v. 7). Judah was stuck in the quicksand of sin, and to the surprise of neither God nor His prophet their downward slide only quickened (v. 7).

"Just as sowing to the Spirit yields such dispositions and states of mind as love, joy, peace, and patience, so, on the other side of the field, sowing to the flesh brings a crop of attitudinal sins and miseries as well as bodily ones. . . . In both instances, the dynamics of sowing and harvesting go on down the ages with awesome inevitability. A main reason is that people not only reap what they sow but also sow what they reap. Abusive parents who then get abused by their children reap what they have sown. But abused children who abuse their children sow what they have reaped. The same goes for terrorized terrorists, swindled swindlers, and jilted lovers who even the score with their next partner. Inside a given human life, the dynamics of sowing, reaping, and resowing lie behind the process of character formation." Cornelius Plantinga Jr., *Not the Way It's Supposed to Be: A Breviary of Sin* (Grand Rapids: Eerdmans, 1995), 69–70.

God's response was to call on Judah to "wait for me" (v. 8). The psalmists had taught God's people how to wait for Him to deliver them from trouble (e.g., Ps. 27:13–14; 37:34; 38:15). Now Zephaniah said, "Wait . . . for God to *bring* you trouble!" Zephaniah pictured the inhabitants of Jerusalem and those of the entire earth perishing together on the day of the Lord. Having forsaken God, Judah had lost its distinctiveness as a people. Choosing to live *in* the ways of the world, they now had to accept the results which came with being just another part *of* a depraved world.

- *Zephaniah began (1:2–3) and ended (3:8)*
- *his prophecy of judgment by picturing the*
- *destruction of Judah as if the entire earth*
- *were being swept away. The incessant and*
- *stubborn corruption of sin demanded nothing*
- *less. Could hope survive?*

THE DAY OF THE LORD AS A DAY OF HOPE (3:9–20)

Judgment was coming, but by God's grace it was not the final word. Zephaniah saw another day of the Lord when God would purify His people and restore them to favor with Him.

A Day of Conversion (vv. 9–13)

Looking beyond judgment, Zephaniah saw a day when not only Judah but "all peoples" would turn to God. He described this day in terms of themes or events mentioned earlier in the Bible:

- God was going to "change [all peoples'] speech into a pure speech" so that everyone could "call upon the name of the

"But the fruit of the Spirit is love, joy, peace, patience, kindness, goodness, faithfulness, gentleness, self-control; against such there is no law. And those who belong to Christ Jesus have crucified the flesh with its passions and desires" (Gal. 5:22–24, RSV).

Lord" (v. 9). Zephaniah apparently had in mind the story of the tower of Babel (Gen. 11:1–9).The builders of the tower had wanted to make a "name" for themselves (Gen. 11:4), indicating their desire for self-impowerment and control. God instead changed their language and dispersed them over the face of the earth. A reversal of this event would allow people to have the kind of fellowship with God that He had intended all along, and to call upon *His* name instead of trying to establish their own.

- As in the days of Solomon, peoples from across the world would be drawn to God, bringing offerings and gifts to Him (v. 10; cp. 1 Kings 10:1–10; Isa. 19:18–25; Zech. 14:16–19; Mal. 1:11; Matt. 2:1–12).

- Mankind would no longer be bound by the effects of sin and shame that had plagued humanity since the Garden of Eden (v. 11; cp. Gen. 2:25–3:7).

- People would act in a manner that was truly pleasing to God, with humility, righteousness, truthfulness, and a desire to seek His ways, just like the great saints of old (vv. 12–13; cp. Gen. 6:9; Num. 12:3; Mic. 6:8).

- Zephaniah saw that God's people would "lie down in pastures" and never be afraid, a picture reminiscent of Psalm 23 (v. 13; cp. Ps. 23:2).

Zephaniah's description presupposes a change of heart which results in changed behavior. Simply put, he saw a day when people from all nations, not just Israel or Judah, would be saved. The result would be a transformed society. The New Testament teaches that God brings about this kind of change only through

Jesus (John 1:12–13; 10:10; Rom. 6:1–11; 2 Cor. 5:17).

- *Zephaniah saw a day when God would cre-*
- *ate a new people who would seek after Him*
- *in righteousness and truth. This prophecy is*
- *coming true as people find new life in Christ.*

A Day of Restoration (3:14–20)

Zephaniah concluded his prophecy by describing how God would restore His people once He had changed their hearts so they wanted to follow Him. He called for Israel to "sing aloud" because their enemies had been defeated (vv. 14–15, RSV). Their time of judgment was over; and, with God as their victorious king, they no longer needed to fear evil (vv. 15–17). Zephaniah's call to sing is reminiscent of the royal enthronement festivals of the Judean monarchy (cp. 3:18). It looked forward to the revived faith in God that characterized the Jews when they returned from the Exile. It also points to an inward freedom from sin such as Zephaniah described in 3:9–13.

"Daughter of Zion" and "daughter of Jerusalem" (3:14) are common Old Testament phrases that refer to the inhabitants of Jerusalem (cp. 2 Kings 19:21; Song of Sol. 3:11; Lam. 2:1; etc.). The "daughters of Judah" (Ps. 97:8) and "daughters of the Philistines" (Ezek. 16:27) were the cities and villages of Judah and Philistia, and also their inhabitants.

The last two verses of Zephaniah foresee the time when the Jews would return from Babylonian Exile and be reestablished in their homeland. They also point to the outpouring of God's blessing on all people who turn to Him. Zephaniah used physical maladies to describe Judah's helpless predicament (v. 19); Jesus referred to a similar passage from Isaiah to announce the beginning of His own ministry (Luke 4:18–19; cp. Isa. 61:1–2). Through God's work of restoration, Judah would become "renowned and praised among all the peoples of the earth" (v. 20, RSV; cp. Deut. 26:18–19).

■ *God promised to return His people to favor*
■ *and bless them in their land. He did this for*
■ *ancient Israel when He brought His people*
■ *back from Babylonian Exile. Through Jesus,*
■ *God brings similar blessings to His people*
■ *today.*

QUESTIONS TO GUIDE YOUR STUDY

1. How did Zephaniah draw on earlier biblical events to explain what was going to happen to Judah?

2. How is it possible to point out sin without alienating the sinner?

3. How can time-bound prophecies made to ancient Israel and Judah have relevance for Christians today?

******

On the day that I finished writing the portion of this study guide covering the book of Nahum, I attended a wedding at the Syrian Orthodox Church in Bethlehem, Israel. The ceremony was conducted in Aramaic, the language of Jesus. When standing in line to congratulate the newly married couple, one of the clergymen commented that his family, who live in northern Iraq, could trace their ancestry to Nineveh, the ancient capital of the Assyrian Empire. Suddenly the immensity of time and space collapsed into the here and now, as the past touched the present. Here was a descendant of ancient Nineveh—the city that was the epitome of evil in the eyes of the biblical writers—who looked to Jesus for life and faith. What a wonderful picture of God's reconciling work among the nations! The biblical prophets foresaw a day when God's saving grace would extend through Israel to all the peoples of the earth. By taking their words to heart, we, too, can learn what it is that God requires of us, and how to "do justice, and to love kindness and to walk humbly with our God" (Mic. 6:8, RSV).

******

The following is a collection of Broadman & Holman published reference sources used for this work. They are provided here to accompany the reader's need for more specific information or for an expanded treatment of the books of Jonah, Micah, Nahum, Habakkuk, and Zephaniah. All of these works will greatly aid the reader's study, teaching, and presentation of the Bible's prophetic books.

Barker, Kenneth L. and Waylon Bailey. *Micah, Nahum, Habakkuk, Zephaniah* (The New American Commentary, vol. 20). A scholarly treatment that emphasizes the text of Micah, Nahum, Habakkuk, and Zephaniah, their backgrounds, theological considerations, issues in interpretation and summaries of scholarly debates on important points.

Cate, Robert L. *An Introduction to the Old Testament and Its Study*. An introductory work presenting background information, issues related to interpretation, and summaries of each book of the Old Testament.

Dockery, David S., Kenneth A. Mathews, and Robert B. Sloan. *Foundations for Biblical Interpretation: A Complete Library of Tools and Resources*. A comprehensive introduction to matters relating to the composition and interpretation of the entire Bible. This work includes a discussion of the geographical, historical, cultural, religious, and political backgrounds of the Bible.

Farris, T. V. *Mighty to Save: A Study in Old Testament Soteriology*. A wonderful evaluation of many Old Testament passages that teach about salvation. This work makes a conscious attempt to apply Old Testament teachings to the Christian life.

Francisco, Clyde T. *Introducing the Old Testament*. Revised Edition. An introductory guide to each of the books of the Old Testament. This work includes a discussion on how to interpret the Old Testament.

Holman Bible Dictionary. An exhaustive, alphabetically arranged resource of Bible-related subjects. An excellent tool of definitions and other information on people, places, things, and events mentioned in the Bible or forming the historical context of the Bible.

Holman Bible Handbook. A summary treatment of each book of the Bible that offers outlines, commentary on key themes and sections, illustrations, charts, maps, and full-color photos. This tool also provides an accent on broader theological teachings of the Bible.

Holman Book of Biblical Charts, Maps, and Reconstructions. This easy-to-use work provides numerous events and drawings of objects, buildings, and cities mentioned in the Bible.

Kelley, Page H. *Micah, Nahum, Habakkuk, Zephaniah, Haggai, Zechariah, Malachi* (Layman's Bible Book Commentary, vol. 14). A popular-level treatment of the books of Micah, Nahum, Habakkuk, Zephaniah, Haggai, Zechariah, and Malachi. This easy-to-use volume provides a relevant and practical perspective for the reader.

Sandy, D. Brent, and Ronald L. Giese Jr. *Cracking Old Testament Codes: A Guide to Interpreting the Literary Genres of the Old Testament*. This book is designed to make scholarly discussions available to preachers and teachers.

Smith, Billy K. *Hosea, Joel, Amos, Obadiah, Jonah* (Layman's Bible Book Commentary, vol. 13). A popular-level treatment of the books of Hosea, Joel, Amos, Obadiah, and Jonah. This easy-to-use volume provides a relevant and practical perspective for the reader.

Smith, Billy K., and Frank S. Page. *Amos, Obadiah, Jonah* (The New American Commentary, vol. 19B). A scholarly treatment that emphasizes the texts of Amos, Obadiah, and Jonah, their backgrounds, theological considerations, issues in interpretation and summaries of scholarly debates on important points.

Smith, Gary V. *The Prophets as Preachers: An Introduction to the Hebrew Prophets.* An examination of the impact of the prophets and their writings on contemporary Christians. This book is an excellent college or seminary level textbook and a comprehensive resource for pastors and other serious Bible students.

Smith, Ralph L. *Old Testament Theology: Its History, Method, and Message.* A comprehensive treatment of various issues relating to Old Testament theology. Written for university and seminary students, ministers, and advanced lay teachers.

SHEPHERD'S NOTES

_____

_____

_____

_____

_____

_____

_____

_____

_____

_____

_____

_____

_____

_____

_____

_____

_____

_____

_____

_____

_____

_____

_____

SHEPHERD'S NOTES

SHEPHERD'S NOTES